PLETHORA

THE NEVER-ENDING BEGINNING

OSCAR "OFOESHO" ROBERTS

PLETHORA

The Never-Ending Beginning

Love, Drugs, Hustle and Pain
Story about my life through jail and God

TABLE OF CONTENTS

PROLOGUE

Three days shy of an 18-month journey...

In April 2015 I was sentenced to 28 months in Federal prison. Almost 2 years later, I sit on my top bunk as I stare around me out the window at the ocean and the large ship unloading cargo.

I went from a high-rise facility in downtown Los Angeles, to a medium security facility in Victorville, California, to this low-security facility in San Pedro California, called Terminal Island.

Even though my time in prison is light compared to most of my fellow inmates, I've suffered the same as many of us. My fiancé left me 6 months into my time in jail, friends either turned their backs completely or resorted to spreading rumors. I've seen people fight. I've seen people die. I woke up to my cellmate slicing his wrist and neck in the middle of the night.

Yet in all of this neglect and evil, I have grown so much closer to Jesus Christ and my family. I still have a few real friends in the free world.

As I ran all of this through my mind, I began to have thoughts about my entire life, especially my love life and the many times I've been left by women I thought I loved.

While incarcerated, I said a few things to myself. First, I said I definitely made bad choices for the women I tried to love. And second, I said a little bit of all of this with my other life experiences would make an amazing novel.

So here I am opening up this overflowed box of memories, experiences, choices, love, drugs, hustle and a lot of pain. Which is actually the title of this memoir of my life.

Love represents God, who was there from the beginning and is still here now.

Drugs not only represent the obvious but also represent sex and women who were more of an addiction for me than any drug I ever consumed.

Hustle represents my drive and ability to survive in so many hopeless situations.

Pain represents too much to write. But you will definitely be able to tell if you embark on this journey with me how much I've endured and how much I've dished out to others.

So let me take you back about 37 years to my birthplace of Richmond, Virginia and how I ended up a Southern California representative with a passion for family, music, and most importantly, LOVE.

I call this part the, "son I thought I was" before it all got fuzzy and changed into confusion and denial.

CHAPTER 1

THE SON I THOUGHT I WAS

Ralph Waldo Emerson wrote these words. "I am nothing. I see all. The currents of the Universal Being circle through me. I am part or parcel of God."

My plan today was to write later this evening on my bed but my bunkmate Steve presented me with some ideas and motivation after reading the first two pages. He advised me to look into the author Ralph Waldo Emerson.

My bunkmate is a very intelligent man in his 50s. For me being a Black inmate and him being White, and also him being incarcerated for child pornography, we make an odd team. But with God, all things are possible. He and I have developed a very strong brotherly bond. I thank God for him and pray for him daily. I'm glad I had the opportunity to know him, hear his story and not judge him for his involvement in his crime, like a lot of other inmates do.

This novel is becoming more with each second that passes by and my heart is tugged with emotions and excitement at the same time as I recollect my life experiences. Let me tell you a little bit about my early childhood and my parents.

As I mentioned earlier, I was born in Richmond, Virginia at MCV hospital on March 13th, 1978 to a young teenage mother and an older father- or so I thought- but we will get into that later.

My parents are from Petersburg, Virginia. They are both from very large families. They both had a total of 10 siblings. Both of my parents are Christians and come from a family of believers. Out of both my parents' families, my father's family seemed to be the strictest. Papa is a Vietnam Veteran. He graduated from Virginia Commonwealth University. My mother finished high school, maintained a job, and raised me with my father. For as long as I can remember they have been in love with each other and they still are to this day.

You would think I would have turned out better in my romantic missions, but obviously at 38 years old with 5 children from 5 different women, one false marriage and another failed marriage, I never found anyone to fulfill me the way they fulfill each other.

On December 27th, 1980 my baby sister was born. She instantly became Daddy's little girl.

The most vivid thing I can remember about that time was the Christmas before we moved to Los Angeles, California. That Christmas was amazing. I was given so many presents. My favorite was a red tricycle I loved to ride.

I shake my head as I look around remembering lots of happy and fun family moments. Why did I allow so many bad things to influence me into these multiple jail experiences and numerous sexually charged moments in time?

So let's get back to my childhood…

Virginia was nice from what I can remember. My mother's family loved me a lot. I don't remember ever spending time with my father's family much. I do remember him taking me to school with him and going to rehearsal sessions with his singing group, Stone Fantasy, and watching him sing and sweat a lot. My father was and still is a great singer with a passion for acting and theater. One day he decided to move to Los Angeles with my mom to pursue his entertainment dreams.

My Dad's aunt is the jazz legend Ella Fitzgerald, which would make her my great aunt. But I never got to meet her. By the time I was old enough to realize who she was and connect the dots she had already passed away.

We drove across the country in a Mercury Comet packed with what we could. My parents had a few friends in Culver City and other Los Angeles areas. I remember staying with one of his friends in a nice complex with a swimming pool and I loved to swim. Then we found a place in Inglewood and officially became California residents.

It was a small back house in a mostly Black residential location. We only stayed there a few years. Our car was vandalized a few times and our battery was stolen. That's when crack was on the rise. Being from the ghetto in Virginia, my parents decided to move us all to Bellflower, California, a predominantly white area at that time.

My sister and I were attending a private school, W.E.B. Dubois Academic Institute of Crenshaw and 54th Street. I really excelled at that school. I learned French and Swahili in the 2nd grade. But then we were transferred to Washington Elementary, a public school in Bellflower on the same street we lived on, Ryon Ave. We lived in an upstairs downstairs two-bedroom apartment which was a big upgrade from where we last lived. This would be my home until I graduated from high school.

My parents worked very hard to keep me far away from welfare. We became members of the Crystal Cathedral in Garden Grove pastored by the late great Robert Schuller.

My father tried to make it in the entertainment world, but soon lost his appetite for it. That's when I noticed him leaning towards his sales abilities and soon-to-be minister.

It's 11:30 am, June 19th, 2016, Father's Day. I'm sitting here outside on the south yard enjoying a soft breeze masking the hot sun as I stare out at the ocean. I may be in prison but from where I've been now, it's a blessing to be here in itself.

I didn't receive any Father's Day cards from a single soul. Not my mother or father, brothers or sisters, aunts, uncles, friends, or children. I made sure I sent each of them Mother's Day, Father's Day and birthday cards to acknowledge them on their special days–but not a single one for me.

I'm not upset but I am sad. A lot of people don't understand how important a simple piece of mail is to us, convicts.

That's one of the reasons why I can't wait to have my own real family. I've grown to understand so much more about life in this term of imprisonment. Even though I'm sure my family loves me, I think they have a lot to learn about the action of love and the agape aspect of it. Love is unconditional and it's pure.

OK. Enough about today. Let's go back to the past again.

My first crush was this teenage beauty queen named Baldwin. I can still see her beautiful caramel face and pearly white teeth. I was about 8 years old, or maybe even younger, but I had plans for her. The private school I was attending at the time went from kindergarten to 12th grade. No sooner than the moment I discovered my crush, I was transferred to Washington Elementary, a public school in Bellflower, my new home.

Bellflower was a big change for me, mainly because of the number of white people I was exposed to. Due to my friendly personality, it didn't take me long to adjust to my new environment. It was a lot safer.

My previous school was right in the middle of the hood. Just before my transfer, a woman was sitting at the bus stop right across the street from school, with a child in her lap. Her baby was struck in the head by a stray bullet from a drive-by a couple of blocks away.

Life is a precious gift not to be taken for granted.

I hate all this evil that exists in the world. Why can't we all live in peace and harmony? Seriously. We are all human beings. Yes, we all make mistakes. Let's learn from them. We have so many different examples to draw from.

I can say this because I've fallen from grace multiple times but I've never picked up a gun or knife with the intention of killing anyone. I owned a couple of illegally obtained guns but I never used them or kept them long enough. God always pulled me out of that trap.

One of those traps was part of the sentence I'm serving now.

In June 2011, I was arrested in Media, Pennsylvania for having a firearm without a license. I finally resolved that case in February of 2016 while serving my current federal time. I took a deal for 1-2 years that ran concurrent with my current Federal charges.

Back to my childhood….

After my transfer to public school, it took me a while to adjust because right before that, my mother had a terrible car accident that totaled her brand new Toyota Corolla. Around that time my mother got pregnant with one of my younger brothers, Amassis. She decided to start a women's clothing business called Bonnie's Hosiery.

I was torn at that time by my dreams of being an entertainer and instead had to work in the new family business. It started off fun for me because I was a naturally skilled salesman and my people skills were impeccable. As my father would say back then, I could sell ice to an Eskimo.

Our business was mainly Los Angeles based. We would go from Gardena to Compton, South Central, Beverly Hills and even Hollywood to hair and nail salons soliciting our merchandise to the customers as well as the hair and nail technicians.

The business was an instant success. People loved us. It started off as me, my mom and my sister, Shamis. As the years went on, my younger brothers would also become part of the sales team. But none of them were gifted like I was gifted. I would make a minimum of $1,000 a week consistently.

When I was about 9 or 10, my dad was laid off from his job and he became part of our sales force. That's when he and

I started to clash. My dad was very hard on me and my sister. He drilled us with sales tapes from Zig Ziglar, Les Brown and Al Williams. It made me look at all the things I was missing out on as a child. Not that it wasn't good for me. But we would work Monday- Saturday after school until 7 or 8 pm and Saturday from 10 am- 5 pm. Needless to say, I had no childhood. No sports, barely any friends and there was no way I was going to have a career as an actor or singer.

For about a summer before our business took off, I did a few small roles in movies and a TV series but my mother didn't have the patience or time to dedicate to me like that. I've resented her for over 20 years. I've just recently cleared my mind and heart of all that resentment among other things I will touch on later in this story.

So back to my love life…

It was 1988 I believe. I was in 5th grade. Her name was Aisha Johnson and she had this young boy sprung. I would write love poems and little notes to myself about her. Then one day my heart grew and I wrote her a note. It said, "Would you be my girlfriend?" There was a "yes" and "no" box attached.

To my surprise, she marked, "yes.

We met up after school briefly before I had to go to work with my family. She gave me a kiss and said, "Don't tell anybody." It seemed strange to me but I said OK. I skipped all the way home.

The next day I saw her and I was all smiles. But she was with her friends. I was so excited I confided in one of my friends O'Neal Forbes. "Guess what, bro? Aisha is my girlfriend."

He obviously didn't believe me and told people. By the time school was almost over people were teasing me. Then the bomb was dropped. Aisha apparently denied it. Then she approached me and ended it officially. Me and my big mouth.

I was devastated. That heartbreak kept me away from girls officially until my senior year in high school.

I had small crushes here and there. But nothing materialized into anything.

Then I met Cristina. She was Filipino. She might have been a freshman or a sophomore. I can't fully remember but she was beautiful and she was my first real girlfriend.

I was still a virgin and the youngest senior at 16 years old. I was a year ahead because I skipped 1st grade at my private school.

Cristina was a lot more experienced than I was but I was too blind to see it.

Today is Monday, June 20th, 2016. I've been locked up for 18 months today officially.

I just finished doing my morning readings. I start with *Purpose Driven Life* by Rick Warren. Then my daily devotional and *Life Principle Bible* by Charles Stanley and my NKJV study Bible. I do this to show obedience to God and His Word and to refill my body with positivity.

One of the books I read talks about Philippians 2:5-10. I've put the beginning verse to memory. "Let this mind be in you which was also in Jesus Christ." My goal is to have the mind of Jesus. That's one of the reasons I've completely cut vulgarity out of my vocabulary. I don't even use the "N" word anymore.

I grew up around a lot of cussing, my mother being one of my biggest influences, as well as many of the kids at my school. It didn't take long for me to pick up on those forms of expressing myself. Soon I was cussing like a sailor.

I made a decision in 2014 that I would eliminate those words out of my vocabulary. Actually, speaking like that makes me feel foolish. Now I'm not going to judge anyone and I hope no one stops reading my story due to missing graphic terminology. But I believe I can share my life with you without opening up that window so many people use to throw out trash. Call this my way of doing community service and keeping it clean. I would like my children and other young people to be able to read about the wrong choices I've made, and some of the right choices as well, without being subjected to that type of language.

So let me get back to Cristina…

We had a public relationship, the whole nine. Holding hands on the way to class, kissing, hugging, and walking her home. It took a little while before I started hearing rumors about her and noticing certain characteristics about her.

Due to my close family and somewhat sheltered life, I couldn't really read people properly. My family is very close. We go to church every Sunday. We work together six days a week. We were each other's best friends and everything. Not that any of that was wrong, but for me becoming a man and dealing with hormones was pretty difficult at first.

My father was really strict and we were kids who got spanked. During the 7 years or so after he lost his job and worked in the family business, we would clash from time to time.

I developed a pretty big ego because I was my mother's#1 salesman. Because of that, I felt my father should respect me as the breadwinner. But really, I was hurting myself.

That was part of the reason why he and I didn't talk about girls. I didn't have any real friends. I assumed my life was just like a lot of young men at the time but boy *was* I wrong.

These days my mother and father are the most important people in my life. It took me about 20 years to get to this level.

From my senior year in high school until before I came to jail, I turned into a sex crazed, gang banging, drug dealing, pimpin' and pandering, an extra aggressive thief who didn't care about anyone but himself.

My problems stemmed from trust.

See. Cristina wasn't just my girlfriend. She was available to other guys as well and that broke my heart.

Shortly after my 17th birthday, I ended up losing my virginity to my best friend, Jennifer. Let me tell you–that was the beginning of the end for me.

I had found out Cristina was being sexual with multiple boys and Jennifer confirmed it. I remember Jennifer and I walking home. She came to my house–well, apartment. For some odd reason, my parents weren't home and we decided to have sex in my parent's living room.

I didn't know what I was doing. But she was experienced. It was done 3-5 minutes later. I wasn't a virgin anymore. But I also wasn't anywhere near innocent, either. Jennifer and I never talked again. Even though our sexual episode wasn't what I envisioned it to be, I wanted to feel a connection as much as possible.

You know that saying, "The Lord works in mysterious ways." Well, I can testify to the absolute truth to those words.

I just came from my Monday night Bible study with Brother Mallard. He's a federal inmate from San Francisco with a strong gift for teaching and presenting God's Word to others.

Today he asked us if we knew what our purpose was. He asked us about our passions and talents. You would think they are all the same or at least tied into each other but they really aren't.

You see, my passions are music and entertainment, but my purpose is to bring glory to God in everything I do. That's one of the reasons I'm sharing my life story in a transparent way. Even if I don't fully understand it, the Holy Spirit inside of me is guiding me to be pure with my words and honest about everything.

As much as I've lied in this lifetime, you will not find one lie in any section of this story. This is therapy for me. I'm digging deep and remembering a lot of happy and painful moments in my life. Hopefully, it will save someone else from going down these roads. I want to be a positive influence on those who have already lived similar lives and made many of the same mistakes I've made.

Even though a lot of this story is about my love life, and/or lack thereof; I'm sharing it for a purpose. You see, sharing this life full of experiences will actually lead me to the woman God has for me. It will be a guide for my children I've fathered in the midst of all these choices and decisions.

I don't regret any of my children or any of my experiences because they made me the man I am today.

Today is June 21st, 2016. It's the first day of summer and boy, is it hot, hot, HOT!

I'm currently in film class waiting for the rest of the class to get here. The teacher is a fellow inmate by the name of John Bowe. He is a film director and writer in the free world.

Today I feel like telling you about some of the fun memories I have with my family. Even though we worked hard, we had some special moments. We didn't play organized sports, but we definitely played them as a family.

My father was a great basketball player and he taught us kids how to play. I developed a pretty nice shot. I really enjoyed playing against my father. We also had little family rituals like Chinese food night and pizza and movie rental night. One of my favorites was Freeze Night. The family would load up in the van in our pajamas. We would go to a fast food drive-thru, get cups of ICE water and throw it on each other with the windows rolled down. Such a simple event, but the fun was real and our love for each other as a family prevailed.

Even though we were poor compared to most of our church members, we never experienced welfare or medical assistance. Not having medical coverage may have hurt me the most later in life when it comes to my dental issues. I think I went to the dentist 2 or 3 times between the ages of 4 and 17. I don't ever remember going to the doctor for a physical. Thank God I was a healthy child. But my parents made it all work.

I believe God has blessed me and my family with great health and many other spiritual gifts. It's a lot easier to look at the positives these days due to my optimistic state of mind.

But between the ages of 14- 17, my life was slowly turning into a nightmare.

You see, my legal name is Oscar Leroy Roberts, but during childhood, my name was Oscar Manzira Shaw and I loved my name. My family in Virginia had rumors about me at the time that I was either adopted, and even worse for me that I was not related to my dad by blood at all. I didn't really allow it to set in but it did have an effect on me.

My senior year in high school was a very strange journey for me. I started experimenting with cigarettes, lost my virginity, lost the taste for the family business, and my father and I didn't like each other very much. It got worse on my graduation day when my father caught me doing something foolish and smacked the life out of me in front of a lot of my peers.

I graduated as Oscar Manzira Shaw from Bellflower High School. My grandmother and Aunt Cynthia flew to California from Virginia and made me a very proud and happy young man. Who would have thought that would be the last time I would see my amazingly beautiful Grandma Mable alive?

The summer came and went. I started hanging out with friends of mine who were active gang members. Some were Crips. Others were Bloods. I also started hanging out with this actor/rapper named Sean Young from Beverly Hills. We instantly became very close friends to the point we called each other cousins.

We actually met because a pretty girl we were both dating, named Raquel, invited us to an event in Beverly Hills. She broke my heart. But she is the reason Sean became a big part of my life up until my current incarceration.

During all of these changes, I was approached by the Air Force due to my high scores on my ADSVAB test. I decided to enlist because my father served in the Air Force as well. He went to Vietnam. I made this decision to impress him because he and I weren't on good terms. I also made this decision because I had started gang-banging with the bloods and I was really in over my head.

Then my life took a very drastic turn.

I was still 17 years old and my military recruiter told me I had to have my parents sign me over into the military. I went to my dad to have him sign the paperwork for me. We started arguing and he said the words that have haunted me for over 20 years. "I am not even your father."

I had already gone through all the military channels and was approved with the name Oscar Manzira Shaw. But my father told me I wasn't his son.

I called my mother and told her what happened. She was silent for a little while. Then she confirmed my fear. She came home, took me out to lunch and told me her side of the story.

She said she was young and my real father wasn't reliable. But what didn't make sense to me was the fact that she gave me his first name, his middle name, and his last name. To this day this is still a mystery to me and I have yet to physically meet my biological father. I spoke to him once when I was in prison in 2003.

I called his mother, my grandmother, Augustine Jones. She and I started talking a little more since I found out about my other family. My father just so happened to be at his mother's house and we spoke for a little while. I really don't remember much about the whole conversation but I do remember him blaming it all on my mother and saying my father who raised me stole me from him.

This situation ruined me for quite some time, plus a few other tragic events I will get to as I share my life with you. One thing is for sure. My father who raised me loves me like I am his own and he has taught me so much about life. I truly respect him a lot more today as I think about how hard it was for him to be a father to a child who wasn't biologically his. That is why he is my hero and why I love this man so much. He is my father and will always be that to me.

I hope that as a reader, you're not going to be annoyed by my delivery in this story about my life and journey. Please understand I've been through so much. I've seen so much. I just want to share as much as I can remember with you all. Plus, I'm in prison and I'm drawing my motivation from God. I'm allowing my spirit to guide me to present you with nothing but the truth.

I went to the Air Force with every intention of serving my country, making my father proud, and getting away from the lifestyle I was beginning on the streets of L.A. This new journey began in 1996. I went through my medical and physical examination and the government put us up in the Bonaventure Hotel in downtown L.A.

That night a bunch of recruits and I had lots of fun and celebrated our last night as regular civilians. The next morning, I was on a plane to Texas headed to the Lackland Air Force base and basic training camp.

The first couple of weeks were OK but there was a lot of racial tension between the drill sergeant and me and some of the recruits and me. Even though I was used to and aware of racism, it had been a while since I was treated unfairly.

One of the last times I remembered before that was when a white kid who lived down the street from me in Bellflower spotted me as he was riding past me on his bicycle. I was livid and disgusted. I knocked him off his bike and we fought. We were quickly interrupted by a neighbor who had noticed us tussling.

Basic training was tough for me and the drill sergeant was extra hard on me. I did everything I was supposed to do but it just wasn't enough. I was still young and naive so I just tried harder. I was used to hard work from the family business and discipline instilled in me by my father.

After a big workout and competition, we went back to the barracks for inspection. I failed and got recycled for one week. That meant I had to do an extra week in boot camp. I was upset because I was only a week away from graduating.

As frustrated as I was, I accepted it and moved to a different unit but the drill sergeant was even worse. This time, the drill sergeant was a Caucasian woman who was friends with my previous drill sergeant. She was short-tempered and within 2 days I was recycled again and transferred to the reject unit awaiting final disposition.

A week later the rejects and I were given a general discharge with the option to re-enter at a later time. I was embarrassed and in shock because I couldn't believe how unfairly I was treated and how defenseless I was in this whole ordeal.

They sent me home and my childhood friend Will Jones picked me up from the airport, along with a new friend, Sean

Young. I vaguely remember what we did but I do remember getting back home.

I had got in pretty good shape in boot camp and this part has stuck with me throughout the years. My family was somewhat happy to see me but I was in a very different state of mind. I was still dealing with the lie my parents had me living with and my anger flowed internally. I wanted to be on my own and get as far away as I could. That's when the devil really started having his way with my life.

I started gang-banging and hustling. I also started chasing women and falling in and out of love often. My heart has always been gentle, but it didn't do any good with all the resentment and personal frustrations I harbored.

The guys that introduced me to being a blood were Brian and Lil Man. They were from a pretty big hood in Inglewood. Both of these guys were making money and driving luxury cars. They just appealed to my needs at that point in life.

I first met Brian in Bellflower. We were both going to college in Norwalk. He was a laid back super sneaky brother but we became good friends. Then he introduced me to Lil Man who was a very active gang member and super ladies' man. He and I became very close, very fast. I truly believed these guys were my boys and we did a lot together.

Before I was officially a blood, I was claiming to be one already. Then one day after one of the young homies' funeral at Queens Park, I made the decision to get put on the hood. Little did I know that I picked a really bad time because a lot of the guys were drunk and high. They beat me pretty bad but I held my own and didn't get knocked out. But I think I lost a tooth.

Lil Man was a very respected member of our gang. He's the one who said I had enough. Now I was officially a blood.

Due to my upbringing and the knowledge that I had; I chose not to be like a lot of the others. I was into making money and sleeping with as many women as I could.

My family and I were growing further apart so I moved to Beverly Hills to stay with Sean Young and his mom, Diane. Sean was a child actor and a rapper. He went to Beverly Hills High School and introduced me to a lot of celebrities and children of celebrities, aka "rich kids." I loved this world because I wanted to be a rapper and actor my whole life.

Sean and I became so close we told everyone we were cousins. Even though I smoked a little weed before, Sean and I smoked it all the time. One of our big sources was his mom's stash because she was a marijuana smoker as well. When she would go to work, Sean would go into her room and get her little box from under the bed. It included rolling papers, other utensils, and of course, Mary Jane.

We had big dreams and we also had lots of ladies.

My second real girlfriend was introduced to me by Sean and his on-again, off-again girlfriend, Nicole Brown. Her name was Camie. She was a beautiful Caucasian girl from Brentwood with red hair, a freckled face and a gorgeous smile.

She lived in a mansion with a full court basketball setup and a tennis court. Her family was very traditional in their culture but Camie was not. She was a hip-hop dancer who loved everything urban. We had an instant connection and to this day, I can say she was the closest thing to a real relationship I ever had.

We had fun together and a genuine love built from there but Sean's influence at the time would cause me to make one of the worst decisions I've ever made.

You see, Sean and Nicole had a very toxic relationship. They cheated on each other and would never really forgive each other. This dysfunction didn't affect Camie and me that much in the beginning, but as time passed by, it played a vital role in our breakup.

My ego also became a problem because of the caliber of women I was able to acquire. So many different levels of the opposite sex. I was like a kid in a candy store. This made it difficult for my current relationship with Camie.

Now that I think of it with a clear mind, Sean was jealous of what we had and he wanted me to be miserable with him. We would do everything together. He was my best friend. I trusted him.

It was Christmas time. Camie and I were still together. I had a lot of other women I was dealing with but none of them meant nearly as much to me as she did.

A few days before Christmas, Sean approached me with a very odd proposition. Due to my financial status of being "broke," he advised me to break up with Camie right before Christmas. I don't know what caused me to listen to this ridiculous idea, but I did what he suggested and it broke Camie's heart.

Come to find out she had bought me multiple presents, including some shoes I wanted from Footlocker, which she ended up giving away to a homeless guy. I can't say I'm still living with regrets, but I will admit, I've never forgotten Camie and my heart suffered tremendous pain due to my choices.

I made a couple of attempts to get her back in my life, but none of them were successful. She was done with me. So I started chasing my dream of being an entertainer. I began doing various things to get money.

I also developed connections with some of the people I met in Beverly Hills. One who had a big impact on me was Evan Bogart, the son of an industry mogul who died in the early 80's. Evan lived in Beverly Hills on Camden Drive with his mother, step-father, sister, and a live-in maid. He and I became such good friends I even lived with him for a few weeks to give Sean and his mom a break.

Evan was a talented songwriter and he was also trying to produce music. We would write songs in his room and just have fun. One day, we were trying to figure out what my rap name would be. O-Dog was played out to me. Then a light bulb went off in my head. I was like, "What about O-FOE-SHO? Evan and Sean really liked the idea. From that day on, my entertainment name has been, OFOESHO.

CHAPTER 2

Even though I'm not a big celebrity and I haven't put out any#1 hits, I've definitely made a serious mark on a lot of other stars, superstars, and industry executives.

Today, Evan is a multi-platinum songwriter. One of his biggest hits is S.O.S. by Rihanna. Sean Young is also a pretty big deal with multiple movie roles, TV roles and platinum records with Tupac, Jay Z, Quincy Jones Jr., and Bryson, rest in peace.

I've always had a gift for bringing people together. I never capitalized on it because I never had contracts with anyone.

Remember my childhood friend, Will Jones? This boy had such an amazing voice but no personality. I used to make him sing for people and they would go crazy. I've managed to get us into some major circles but he never believed in himself enough to make it last. I could write about so many of our industry encounters, but I will limit this story to one chain of events that has forged some friendships that still exist for me today.

The legendary rapper/mogul Eazy-E has a daughter named Erin Wright, by the lovely Tracy Jernigen. At the time we met, she was dating Tyron Turner, who played Caine, in the movie *Menace II Society*. He was very good friends with Dalvin and Devonte from Jodeci. Since my boy Will's voice was a cross between KC and JoJo, this new circle we were becoming part of was a very good fit for Will as an artist. Tracy believed in Will and she loved the way I networked. It all started working together. This brought me to a new level of industry individuals.

No disrespect to anyone but this is a very provocative and ghetto style of business. We definitely had some amazing moments together, but Will just didn't believe in himself as much as we believed in him so nothing substantial ever happened for his or my career. But I'm still friends with Tracy and her daughter to this day.

My life story has too many of these stories. What I've shared with you is far from the tip of the iceberg. I will try not to venture off into too many of these particular kinds of stories. From the beginning, my mission was to tell you mainly about my love life and what God has allowed me to learn from every woman I've dated.

With that being said, let me tell you about Amy Carreras. I met her at Universal City Walk. As teenagers, we would go hang out there often to meet girls. I was with Will and Sean when I met her. She was a couple of years younger than me. She had just been dropped off by her parents to see a movie with her girlfriends Meagan Good, Kim Brown and Jamila.

Amy was a Puerto Rican princess to me and for some reason, I was instantly smitten with her. She was from a city in the Valley called Lake View Terrace. I had no idea of the caliber of ladies I was being exposed to but I soon found out the closer I got to Amy. Her parents were doctors, I think, and her friends were either celebrities or the children of celebrities. I'm still friends with Meagan Good and Kim Brown (daughter of football legend Jim Brown) to this day.

Amy and I had a great connection but we were young and she was a couple of years younger than me. She was still a virgin so our relationship was built without sex or sexual encounters.

We would all hang out at Jim Brown's house in the Hollywood Hills. Jim Brown is the one who taught me how to play chess. He carried high expectations for us as children of color. He was and still is a very intelligent man, respected by many. He was also pretty strict with Kim compared to a lot of the other celebrity parents I encountered. But he loved his daughter and treated her friends like his own.

Meagan and her sister Lamaiya, Amy and Jamila, Wesley Jonathon, Ray J, Sean Young, Shorty Mac, Young Buck, Lil J, Raven Symone and many more who are stars and still successful to this day were very close friends of mine at that time. Obviously, God had a different plan for me, but I'm thankful for the lessons I learned and for the good and bad times I had with all of these talented individuals.

As Amy and I got more serious, so did my involvement in the gang I was in and my need for fast money. I started doing check fraud and seeing money I never seen before. But one day I got greedy and sloppy. I tried to cash a check at a check cashing facility that wasn't a bank and got arrested.

I only spent a few weeks in jail. But that was the beginning of the end for me and Amy. Rumor was that she met this guy named Ricky Bell one day when she got out of school in the Valley. Ricky was a member of the group, New Edition.

Even though she answered my calls when I was in jail, I could tell something was different. Eventually, she told me about their relationship. She lost her virginity to him. I was devastated because I really liked her a lot. Even though I loved her. Apparently, it wasn't meant to be.

Later in life she and Ricky got married. They are still together to this day. God works in mysterious ways. That statement is totally factual.

It's amazing to me how life happens. I'm sitting in federal prison, being ordered around like a slave, with low regard. But my history is like a movie. When I share it with some of the guys here, they think I'm lying.

This weekend is the BET awards. Ray J is hosting the weekend events. I'm just like, wow. This man stays relevant in the business and is always promoting something new. Others in my position would be jealous. If I didn't know Jesus the way I do now, I would even be a little disturbed. Instead, I'm proud of him. He's engaged to be married. He has business ventures that seem to be successful and I believe he knows the Lord. All I can do is pray for him and hope his heart is in the right place. I also hope we can reconnect again and rebuild a solid friendship.

I still have dreams and hope to pursue them when I get out of here. It's never too late to achieve what you want. In this day and age, anything is possible, especially with God.

Now back to my love life, or lack of love.

I went back to jail again for another check and I got out. My heart was becoming colder. I was just living day to day.

I used to go to different college campuses to meet girls. This particular day I was at Cal State Northridge hanging out with a couple of friends who went there. That's when I met Sheila, an exchange student from Italy. She was beautiful and we instantly fell for each other. She was Catholic and a virgin. She was waiting for marriage and I respected her decision. That didn't mean I didn't try to change her mind but she was very strong-willed.

It was the summer and we spent a month straight together. We went to see the sights in Hollywood and Beverly Hills. We went shopping and to multiple restaurants. Her friends were all from Italy as well. They really liked seeing us together.

Throughout this time, I was still staying with Sean Young but I also stayed with Sheila at the dorms. We would talk about the future. She would teach me a little Italian, I would help her with her English, and we would just enjoy each other's company.

She came from a wealthy family in a town called Bologne and she loved and respected her family.

At this time, I was very upset with my mother and father. I didn't talk to them much in those days. My bitterness brewed from the previous blow my father laid on me about not being my biological father right before I left for the Air Force. He and my mother were liars in my eyes. I didn't trust them or respect them at that particular time in my life. That's why I lived like a nomad. But Sheila made me feel different.

One night, before I was set to go stay with Sean for a couple of days, Sheila and I laid out on a blanket by the basketball courts. We looked at the stars and talked about our lives and our future together.

I get chills when I think about it now. Two days after this night, she and I would become a distant memory.

Sean had recently got his driver's license and a new all black Nissan Altima with leather seats. He came to pick me up. I gave Sheila a bunch of kisses goodbye. We made plans to see each other soon.

A day later, Sheila was in Los Angeles hanging out with friends but she really wanted to see me. It was late, almost midnight, and Sean's mom didn't like us going out too late. Sheila called Sean's house phone and asked for me. Sean passed me the phone and she asked me if she could come over. I explained Miss Diane's rules and told her I would come to see her tomorrow with Sean.

I could tell she was sad. But before she got off the phone, she said, "Oscar. I want you to know that I love you."

The way she said it made me fall even deeper with her. I told her, "I love you, too." I promised I would see her soon.

As I hung up the phone, I had a very strange feeling. It's difficult to explain. I felt like I was saying goodbye forever.

The next morning Sean and I were woken up by the phone ringing. Sean answered and passed the phone to me. When I grabbed the phone and put it to my ear, I could hear a lot of people crying and talking to each other. The voice that I eventually recognized was the R.A. from Sheila's dorm. With a tremble in his voice, he asked me to turn on the news.

He informed me Sheila was killed in a head-on collision on the 405 freeway. She was a passenger in a car that came into contact with a driver who decided to enter the freeway the wrong way and play chicken with the oncoming traffic.

I couldn't believe what he was telling me. But then reality hit when the news anchor spoke about a foreign exchange student killed on the 405 freeway.

I ended the phone call with the resident advisor. I just lay there in disbelief. Even though our relationship was short-lived, her death had an impact on my life to this day.

A few months passed by. I started spending a lot of time with my friend, Brian. Brian pretty much introduced me to the gang-banging thing by connecting me to Lil Man who had become one of my closest friends at that time. Brian was a lot different than Lil Man. He was a lot more business-minded and very sneaky.

Brian introduced me to a new circle of Black entrepreneurs: Slush, Pretty Tony, Mack, Vincent, Wayne and this other big light-skinned brother who was actually a Crip. Four of these guys were pretty wealthy. They were involved in medical billing and had a bunch of clinics around the L.A. area. Apparently, Brian was next in line to be inducted into this new business.

The money was instant. One day, Brian was driving an old car. Within a week, he was driving a brand new Lexus SC 400 money green with 20-inch Lorenzo rims. His whole image changed from regular styles to Versace and Bruno Mali's, snake skin and ostrich skin shoes.

Being the ladies' man of the crew, I was the go-to guy to provide women to feed their sexual appetites. That's when I first got introduced to the pimp game.

Lil Man didn't like me not getting paid properly for what I was doing so he took control of the situation. He started making the guys pay us for providing women. I had very little interest in this life. I wanted to get involved in the business they were involved in. So I started building individual relationships with key players like Vincent and Pretty Tony. I tried to get close to Slush, the richest one of them all, but he had too much going on already.

Slush had a mansion in Calabasas, a very big house in Palmdale, a Viper, 3 or 4 different Benzes and a whole lot more. Pretty Tony had a record label called TY Entertainment, a recording studio, multiple homes, a couple of Mercedes Benzes and a very low-key way of operating. Vincent was Slush's brother-in-law. He has a mansion in the Diamond Bar, an M3 Beamer, a Mercedes and a villa in Mexico. Vincent also had the biggest appetite for women.

Vincent and I were the first to get pretty close. I would make runs with him to different medical clinics to pick up envelopes full of money and he would let me drive the Beamer or Mercedes. Eventually, he invited me to move into the gated community with him in Diamond Bar.

He loved my ability to get women to come over and do anything we asked them to do. We did a lot together and he taught me a lot about the business but he never took me to the next level. He definitely exposed me to a different life, taking me with him to Mexico and trusting me with his home and his vehicles.

Vincent had many insecurities. He would fall in love pretty quickly. That eventually caused trouble in our friendship. One day, out of the blue, he put me out of his house for no reason at all and I have never seen him since. Now I was back living with Sean Young and sometimes staying with my parents.

Crenshaw Blvd was the big thing in LA on the weekends. People from all over California would drive down to the boulevard to show off their cars and pick up girls.

One Saturday night, Brian picked me up. The plan was to go hit the Shaw and get some ladies. Of course, it was easy to do in his brand new Lexus.

We made this trip often, but this day was different. This Saturday was the day I would meet Shamika Robinson, the future mother of my firstborn son, my first serious relationship and the longest.

Me and my boys were driving up and down Crenshaw Blvd, showing off and flirting with the ladies. As we got closer to the Liquor Bank on Stocker, we noticed a car full of girls driving a Pontiac Grand Prix. Chemistry flowed back and forth until we decided to pull over and get better acquainted.

We pulled into the parking lot of the Crenshaw Mall. I immediately exited the Lexus and locked eyes on this light-skinned black princess with an amazing smile and athletic physique. We talked for a little while and exchanged phone numbers. I was very interested in Shamika, but I was also a player with a lot of women at my disposal.

Shamika and I talked for a couple of months and really started to like each other. She and her cousin planned to come to LA from Lancaster, where they lived. They picked me up from my parents' house in Bellflower and took me back to Lancaster with them. Shamika and I couldn't keep our hands off each other.

Even though my view on sex before marriage has changed due to my understanding of what God expects of us. For me, that first night with Shamika was magical. We made love literally all night long.

I remember looking out the window at the full moon in a pleasure-filled trance. That was the night we made baby Oscar.

This was the beginning of the ups and downs in our relationship. It was hard because neither one of us had a car and I was just all over the place. I was literally living in four different places. I stayed in Long Beach with my childhood friend, Sineca and his mother. I stayed with Sean Young. I stayed with my boys Dion and Dermaine aka Goldie and Deranged and I kind of stayed with my parents as well.

I was making money doing multiple forms of illegal activities and I smoked a very large amount of marijuana. I was also recording music at a few studios, perfecting my craft as a rap artist. I really had talent. I formed a group with Goldie, Deranged and Bad Habit called Cavey Express.

As I sit here in prison remembering all of these moments, I thank God I survived this error of madness. I've always been a loyal friend, but many of my friends weren't loyal to me. I didn't see it clearly at the time. But I definitely see it now.

Shamika and I talked often. And we saw each other a few times. One day when we planned to see each other, she came to Sineca's house in Long Beach with her cousin. I was very excited to see her because I missed her a lot.

As she got out of the car to come with me up the stairs, into Sineca's mom's condo, I noticed this aura around her.

Kind of like a glow. She had told me before she came, she had something important to discuss.

I gave her a few kisses and a very gentle hug and we laid back on the loveseat. As she lay against my chest, she looked me in the eyes and told me she was pregnant with my child.

I instantly got excited and very turned on and we started making love to each other. I'm not proud of this statement, but I've been with a lot of different women. I've had a connection to very few of them the way I had a connection with Shamika. I enjoyed talking to her because she was educated and had dreams and goals like me. She also believed in me and supported me in my musical endeavors.

Needless to say, we decided to have this blessing in the form of a child.

We never even considered an abortion.

Even though Shamika and I were technically together, I still did wrong by her. I was involved with various women and I really didn't think anything was wrong with it. Part of my influence on this promiscuous lifestyle was my circle of friends. Most of them had girlfriends and wives and none of them were faithful. I mean absolutely none. We all live for the next kill like animals.

During Shamika's pregnancy, I didn't see her that much, mainly because we lived so far from each other. Also during that time, I was extremely focused on developing my craft as a rap artist. I was recording with my group Cavey Express aka Cavi Thugs. Also, I was working with my boys Darin and Keon from Cerritos. Darin was a producer. Keon was a rapper. They were also professional car thieves.

Darin is the one who introduced me to one of my longest crushes, Maritza, who he actually used to date. Maritza was an aspiring singer, a model and a video vixen. She was in a music group managed by Mario Wynans that included Candace and Michaelia Long. Little did I know that Michaelia and I would become heavily involved in a very toxic relationship a few years later.

OK. So back to Shamika and my firstborn son.

I was at the studio with Darin working on some records and word got to me that Shamika went into labor and was taken to Antelope Valley hospital. Darin, being a loyal friend to me at the time, didn't even hesitate to stop everything he was doing and take me on a two-hour drive from Long Beach to Lancaster. Darin was pushing his Land Rover to the max.

I think we made it to the hospital in about an hour and a half. We parked his truck and rushed into the hospital, just like a scene in a movie.

I asked the receptionist what room Shamika Robinson was in. She gave me the room number and a wristband so I could go into the room where she was being prepped to give birth. Just as I approached the room, I heard her screaming. I panicked a little bit, but my excitement preceded my fear.

I opened the door just as my baby boy's hand was visible. There was blood and mucus everywhere. I was extremely disgusted at the sight. I had a flashback to when my mother gave birth to my youngest brother, Tamrin. All I could say was, God is amazing.

Shamika was very happy to see me and I was just as happy to see her. I was going back and forth from holding her hand to in between her legs. She pushed and pushed and pushed and pushed, then I heard my baby boy scream.

My first-born son was here on November 12th, 1998. God blessed me with Oscar Louchee Racee Roberts.

The doctor passed me a pair of surgical scissors and instructed me to cut the umbilical cord. I was very nervous and honored to do this monumental act of love and connection. I will never forget the look of my purple baby boy so full of life and potential. At that moment in time, it was like my life was changed. It was like a new engine had been ignited within me. I had to succeed. I had to provide. I had to figure out my life.

I stayed at the hospital for a few hours. Then I went home to tell my family and friends. Camera phones didn't exist at the time so I would have to wait to show off my baby boy.

About a week later Shamika and Oscar were released. Shamika had her own place by then. I got a ride to her and stayed with her for a week or two. I got picked up by Sean and he took me to the valley to hang out with one of our new friends Jarae and his sister Larece. Jarae and I instantly hit it off because we were both very confident players. Everyone called him Ray so that's what I called him.

My life has always been a whirlwind. I made too many quick decisions too fast.

Anyway, I was in Ray's bedroom and I noticed a picture of one of the most beautiful women I had ever seen. Her name was Valerie Maman. She was Moroccan and she was drop dead gorgeous. I asked Ray about her. He said she was an old fling but she wasn't important anymore. I instantly made it a point of getting in contact with her.

I don't remember exactly how but I got her phone number. I called her, and told her about myself and how I felt when I saw her picture. We ended up talking for about 4 or 5 hours straight. It was one of my longest conversations with any woman. She liked me as well and eventually, we met face to face. It was on from there.

She actually liked me for me. She knew I just had a child. I fell hard for this girl. We spent a lot of time together. Our relationship got so serious so fast that the first time my mother and father met my son, which was about a day before Christmas, Valerie was there as well. She met Shamika and everyone knew this was my woman.

By this time, I had a little production deal with Spot Entertainment and I was trying to get Pretty Tony at TY Entertainment to take me seriously as a rap artist.

I was in love with Valerie and she was in love with me. She was also Jewish and very close to her family. She had a best friend (can't remember her name) but I do remember she was a drug addict who took pills. I thought me and Valerie would last forever but something strange happened.

It was my 21st birthday and she and I had plans. She had the keys to her sister's house so she and I decided to have a romantic night together. She bought me some presents and everything seemed perfect. We made love to each other, relaxed, and just enjoyed the night.

As we were preparing to leave her sister's house, the condom fell into one of her sister's plants. I had no idea this happened. A few days passed by and Valerie and I were on good terms, or so I thought. She called me and was very upset. She said, "What have you done?"

I was confused and became instantly defensive. She said, "My sister found the condom that you left at her house." She said her family was very upset with her.

I told her I had no idea what she was talking about. She became silent. Eventually, she spoke again and said, "It's over."

I became emotionally unstable and started crying and telling her how much I love her. I told her this had to be a mistake but she wasn't having it. After only a few months of being together, we were done and I was devastated. I actually saw a solid future with her. She was the first girl I was totally faithful to besides my high school girlfriend Cristina. But that was nothing compared to what Valerie and I had.

After she left me, I changed for the worse. I got caught stealing by Tony, the CEO of Spot Entertainment. I started doing anything to get money.

One day I was in Paramount with Brian, Mack and Pretty Tony, playing dominoes and drinking Hennessy. Pretty Tony had bought a house in Southridge, a nice community in Fontana. He turned the garage into a nice recording studio with a built-in sound booth and everything else that comes with the territory. He mentioned that he had an extra bedroom and offered it to me.

He had a producer named DJ Don Living there running his studio. Tony admired my ability to connect with people but didn't fully believe in me as an artist. He wanted me to connect him with my boy Sean Young who I had brought around a few times. I called Sean, told him about Tony, and made the official connection between them. I also moved into the house. Tony bought me a cheap old Thunderbird I believe cost him $700.

I was so happy to have a car and a place to call my own. I was also excited to be able to see my son more often and spend time rebuilding with his mother, Shamika.

I was also very persuasive with women at this time. I literally had about 10 different girlfriends and they all loved me.

Ever since Valerie, I vowed to always have a backup plan because I didn't want to be alone. I had issues, but at the time, I couldn't see it.

DJ Don knew some of the same people I did and we got along pretty well. At that time, he was working with the Five Footaz, Warren G's rap group that consisted of Cobra Red, Nehi, Neb Luv and the new edition, Pinky. He also worked with Bad Azz, who was poppin' at the time and J-Money and McGruff. All of these artists and I developed a pretty good connection, especially the girl group.

Cobra Red had a little son just like me. Sometimes I would have my son with me and she would have hers with her, too. His name was Solomon. He was an adorable little boy.

By this time, Sean Young had a production deal with Tony's company, TY Entertainment. He showed off by pulling up on me in Southridge in a brand-new Ford Expedition. Not only him-DJ Don got one, too.

I must admit, I was a little uneasy. I was totally left out of the equation. It's funny to me as I think back. I've introduced Sean to multiple revenue streams and the only one I got any percentage from didn't come until 8 years after the Expedition experience.

I have no regrets, but I learned a lot about true friendship and loyalty. You see, God made us for the purpose of having relationships. That's why love is so important.

It's 10:09 am, June 27th, 2016.

I'm reading this amazing book by Joyce Meyer called, *Battlefield of the Mind.* I'm almost finished reading it. Have to share with you a little section called *"Wilderness Mentality."*

This terminology is referring to the Israelite's 11-day journey that took them 40 years.

This describes the life I'm sharing with you in this story. I should be much further ahead and very successful in life but I took all the wrong roads. Yet God already knew the paths that would lead me back to Him fully aware of His Word.

Joyce Meyer wrote: *The proud man runs in the strength of his own flesh and tries to make things happen in his own timing. Pride says, "I am ready now." Humility says, "God knows best and He will not be late!" A humble man waits patiently. He actually has a "reverential fear" of moving in the strength of his own flesh. But a proud man tries one thing after another, all to no avail. As we have seen, impatience is also a sign of pride and the only answer to pride is humility.*

In sharing these quotes from her book, I would like you to understand this doesn't apply to all. You see, a non-believer can be full of pride and also full of disrespect for others and still be successful when it comes to money, fame, etc. But for us believers who try to live a double-minded life, it will be very difficult for us to achieve much without choosing a temperature. Either you are hot for Jesus or cold for him. There is no room to be lukewarm, especially in this world we live in now. We need to represent God the way an ambassador should.

I'm sitting in prison mainly for rushing instead of waiting and I lost almost everything. I lost my fiancé by coming to jail 9 days after I proposed. I lost friends and a lot of connections as well. But now that my eyes are opened and I'm drug free and sex free not many of them, including her, were good for me.

We were all lukewarm believers trying to manipulate the Lord and fit Him into our schedule instead of allowing Him to lead us. I believe that I will actually succeed in life this time because my heart is finally in the right place and my goals and values are rooted in the Spirit.

Being a Christian is not easy. Especially when you've lived such a sinful life. I've tainted my spirit with all of these women and friends in this life. Also, my multiple drug habits didn't make it any better. But you know what, God still loves me, which means he loves you, too.

This story isn't meant to impress anyone because of all the celebrities I've encountered or all the money I've made. This story is half for you and half for me so I can show my children how much grace God gave their father. I truly can't wait for God to walk me through these gates to physical freedom. I have managed to keep my mind and spirit free through the study of His Word and fellowship with other believers. This has allowed me to be free even while incarcerated.

Here's a word of advice to all those who have never been to jail or arrested. First of all, stay that way. Second of all, don't pass judgment on all convicts. We are human just like you. We just got caught doing whatever wrong we were doing. Many of us have changed. All we want is love and a chance to share love with others.

Life is short and there is already enough hate in the world. How about we be different and bring joy to each other?

OK *now* let's get back to Fontana and the music or lack of it.

Sean and DJ Don had new trucks and basically, I was jealous. In my jealousy, I put my time and energy into women and hustling with Lil Man and Brian. I also spent time with my beautiful baby boy. He was only a few months old, but I could tell he loved his father. He was never a problem, like for real never. He had such peace and joy about himself. I remember our first Christmas together when my Mom met him and I kept him for a few days.

Sean came to pick me up in Altima (this was a few months before he had the truck). We had been invited to Ladera Heights by a female singer friend of ours named Miyoko. Jamila and Ty had a get-together at Miyoko's parents' house. They were signed to music mogul Chris Stokes. The name of their group was Girl. Miyoko had a brother Sean and I were cool with and two super-talented sisters Jenae and Jamila. Nowadays they are known as Mila J and Jenae Aiko and they're pretty successful singers.

The purpose of me telling this story is because this would be my first and last Christmas with my son. That day plays in my head like a movie. Baby Oscar wore this cute red Polo outfit and everyone at the house adored him. His life did so much in such a short time, it's still hard to accept that he's gone.

So here goes more of my stupid decisions that cost me dearly.

I was living pretty well in Southridge. The studio was poppin' and I was really starting to blossom as an artist. I learned a lot from the Five Footaz, J-Money, McGruff, Legacy, Bad Azz, Sean Young and even DJ Don.

One day I was trying to feed our dog. I couldn't find a can opener, plus we needed more dog food. The other day I had made a couple thousand bucks so I wasn't broke. I had one of the guys take me to the grocery store in the pick-up truck we used for errands.

I went into the store and instead of buying everything like I should have, I opted to steal the can opener and some other items. I paid for a few things.

At this particular point in my life, I frequently stole from stores. I was doing check and credit scams so I didn't believe in paying for anything.

The cashier rang up the items I was paying for, bagged them, and I was on my way. As I got to the door, I was approached by their plain-dressed security guard who watched every move I made. I tried to break for it but they overpowered me. They put me in handcuffs and called the police.

I had just got away from a bank where I had almost got caught. I left my ID there so I knew I had a warrant. I gave the police a false name and tried to lie my way out of the situation. The cop took me to my house so he could get my ID because I told him it was there, trying to get out of it. For some reason, everyone in the house told the officer my real name and it was over from there. My warrants came up and I was taken to WVDC (West Valley Detention Center) in San Bernardino.

I was still a gang banger then and I let it be known where I was from. I was placed with the other bloods in jail. This happened in August. Baby Oscar was 9 months old.

I had been to jail a couple of times before, but no longer than a few weeks. This would be my first official bid as we felons call it. My charges were petty theft with a prior because I had been caught stealing before but only given a citation. My other charge for the check fraud was commercial burglary. At this time, I didn't understand the importance of having a paid attorney, so I accepted the assistance of a public defender. I remember thinking to myself over and over again, *if I just paid for the can opener.* What a stupid decision.

After my arraignment, my public defender came to see me. This should have been a red flag because I didn't know the law at all. He told me the prosecutor had a deal for me that would save me from going to prison. He would combine both cases and give me a county year. At that time, it was 8 months and 20 days with good time. Just the mention of prison scared me enough that I signed the deal.

CHAPTER 3

After signing, I called my family and Shamika and gave them the news. My parents didn't like the fact I was in jail period. So, hearing that I was about to do some time didn't help the situation at all. My father being the super spiritual man of God he is tried to give me the best advice he could. But I still had issues with him after discovering he wasn't my dad. My mom was as nice as she could be, but she was also very disappointed.

Now Shamika was totally different. She understood my position due to her own family issues. We reconciled a lot of our past differences and decided to be a couple again and officially be a family again when I got released.

I still had another warrant in LA County for a probation violation but I wasn't worried about that.

Shamika came to visit me with baby Oscar a couple of times. So did my family. It was tough having to see them behind a glass window with no physical contact at all.

This particular jail was very organized and at this time, the Blacks and Hispanics didn't get along much.

OK, let's take a quick break and come back to the present.

As I was sleeping last night I began thinking about this story of my life and a major milestone popped into my head that had been dormant for years. I've been up since 2 am thinking about this event in my life and how I was going to share it with you lovely people. It has to do with my love life, life of love and/or the lack thereof.

Her name is Debra Delshad, my actual first real love, the first real woman I had before Sheila and Shamika.

I had just gotten out of the Air Force, well kicked out, and I was at one of my favorite places to hang out with Sean and Will- The Beverly Center.

At this time, it was the best mall in Los Angeles/Beverly Hills. Everyone shopped there. At any given moment you would see huge celebrities and wealthy people enjoying the facility.

The boys and I were on the prowl looking for girls. I noticed this short and gorgeous woman looking at some items in the Louis Vuitton store. I didn't want to follow her in so I just waited and stared at her while Sean and Will teased me saying she was out of my league. Instead of deterring me from approaching her, this motivated me to put my fears aside and take a leap of faith. Something in my heart said she was special.

As she exited the store, I caught up to her and introduced myself. I asked what her name was. She said, "Debra," in a sweet, satisfied tone that made every hair on my body stand up. We continued to converse and I asked her if I could call her sometime. She said yes and from that day forward, my life would be changed forever.

You see, Debra was technically out of my league. Let me tell you what I remember about her. Her parents were pretty wealthy, from Bel Air or the high end of Beverly Hills. She was in law school, attending Loyola Law. I think she had already graduated from USC. She was older than me. But she was attracted to me and she must have liked my approach. I kissed her hand when I met her and treated her like the queen she was.

I called her often and we would have great conversations. She was a very busy person, but she still made time for me. Our first time together again, she drove her father's Lexus to my mother's house where Sean was with me. She let him drive and she and I sat in the back seat. We went to Redondo Beach and walked on the pier holding hands and adoring each other. Our chemistry was real and she even met my mother.

She had an apartment in the Palms area off the 10 freeway and La Cienega and actually drove a Toyota Celica but was getting a new Lexus when she graduated law school. A couple of times I even hung out with her while she studied at Loyola.

This woman made me feel special but my insecurities began to bother me. I had no car, no job, no steady income and she was used to finer things. We were a couple for a few months but I started getting in trouble a lot and living the wrong lifestyle. Eventually, we drifted apart but remained friends for almost 2 years. I still remember the first 6 digits of her phone number were 310-254.

This part of my life got drowned in drugs and other women and I believe losing her really took me to a dark place. After her, I felt like I settled with many of the women in my life. This relationship isn't regretful but I do wish I got my life together and made her my wife. I would be in a much better place right now and jail definitely wouldn't be one of them.

The moral of this life-changing event is to be mindful of your surroundings and never settle.

I mean all of this is from a Godly standpoint, not worldly. Even though this woman came from wealth, she accepted me for me. She also taught me a lot and I will always respect her for that.

Debra, wherever you are, I hope that you're happy and enjoying your life and rooted in God's Word.

Pastor Warren wrote in his amazing book, *The Purpose Driven Life*, "The best use of life is love. The best expression of love is time. The best time to love is now."

So, answer this: Honestly, are relationships my first priority? How can I ensure that they are?

These quotes were a part of my reading for today and the spiritual irony is that I read this after I wrote the earlier section about Debra. Look, I don't mean to preach to any of you, but if you don't believe in God my advice is to please begin and watch how your life changes.

Do not block the blessings within this story. I have not added or changed anything to please anyone. If anything, I have forgotten so much due to my lifestyle choices and drug habits. But this book, as I've said before, has been so therapeutic. It has allowed me to remember a lot of things that have hurt me and a lot of things that made me happy as well.

So now let's get back to baby Oscar and my first real bid in jail.

In the midst of the racial tension, I ended up getting a job in the kitchen as a meat slicer, working with mostly Mexicans. I had to learn how to use the machine. But once I got the hang of it, I was on my way to prepping the meat for the jail's meals. I did this job for a couple of months and started to build relationships with a few of my fellow inmates. I was also developing my craft as a writer and a poet.

A friend I slept next to noticed me in my element and started asking about my life. We became friends and eventually came up with my first company, called Left Coast Entertainment. We were pretty much motivated by each other and our eagerness to do more with our lives. We would go to church together and read the Bible together. It's sad I don't remember his name but I can say he was a good friend to me then. Eventually, he was released and I still had a few months to do.

I was getting regular mail and visits from Shamika and occasional visits from my family as well. I was very happy about my new mindset and ready to raise my son. At the end of February, I was expecting a visit from Shamika. My mom, father, sister, brothers, and baby Oscar came instead.

Baby Oscar was walking and running all over the place. He was such a happy baby. He would try to kiss me through the glass window separating us, which frustrated him a lot. I will never forget that day because it would be the very last time, I would see my firstborn son alive again.

A few weeks before this visit, I had sliced the tip of my finger off while slicing the meat. I was rushed to medical and patched up by a nurse. I was taken out of the kitchen and put-on leave until I healed up. Then after my wound healed, I got the best job in the jail- working in the O.D.R.- the Officer's Dining Room. I enjoyed this job because of the perks that came with it. Working here meant no more jail food for me. I ate what the officers ate and they ate very well indeed.

After my lovely visit that weekend it was back to work the following week. Everything went well that week and I wrote a few new songs as well. That weekend I didn't get a visit, but it didn't bother me especially because I had a little over a month left and I was ready to begin again. But nothing could have prepared me for that Monday, March 6th, 2000.

I was at work like normal preparing the food when I got called to the warden's office. I went down the long hallway and made my way to his headquarters. I knocked on the door and as I did, I noticed a very sad aura on everyone's faces, especially the warden and his secretary. As I entered his office, I noticed a little note on his desk that said 16 months. I immediately thought I did something wrong or was being accused of doing something wrong and was being given more time in jail.

The warden instructed me to sit down and said I had a phone call. When I put the phone to my ear, I heard a familiar voice crying hysterically on the other end. I immediately knew it was Shamika. I said hello and Shamika said, "Oscar, he's gone."

I said, "Huh?"

She said it again. "He's gone."

I said, "Who's gone?"

Shamika said, "Our baby boy is gone." She explained how he was breathing funny from bronchitis and was given a breathing treatment. The doctor gave him a medicine called Hycoden. It caused his heart to stop and they couldn't bring him back.

I couldn't believe what she had just shared with me. I asked her more questions and we cried together.

I couldn't believe I lost my only child while sitting in a jail cell because of my own selfish needs. All my joy left me. I was mad at God. I almost lost my faith.

The warden and Shamika said they were already working on getting me out of jail so I could bury my child.

It took four days to get me in front of a judge so I could be granted a bereavement pass. Due to my charges being minor compared to others and the hearts of everyone from the warden to the judge, I was granted a one week pass to go and bury my son, then turn myself in to complete my sentence.

That was March 10th, a Friday. I fully remember every detail vividly. My son's funeral was scheduled for that Monday, March 13th which happened to be my birthday as well.

After seeing the judge, I was transported back to the jail. I packed up all of my property and within two or three hours I was released.

A friend of mine that I met in the jail came to pick me up. He lived in San Bernardino which was very convenient. It took us a little over an hour to get to my parents' house in Bellflower. My family was very happy to see me, but the energy in the house was full of mourning. My son's imprint was everywhere; his toys, his clothes, his spirit.

My friend stayed for a few minutes and met my family and then he left to take the long ride back home. Even though I only hung out with him a couple of times since I realize now that God put him in my life for that purpose.

As much as I believe in God, I must admit, that my faith decreased tremendously after the death of my son. Between my father not being my real father and the death of my son, I felt cursed. I often thought, how could God allow this to happen to me?

Let me tell you something real and I mean every word. The devil's mission is to destroy every single human being.

God is 100% love and life is full of many different tests. Death is a guarantee to everyone, some of us sooner than others. Just because my father isn't my biological father, he raised me well and he loves me like his own.

These are my thoughts today, but it's honestly been a struggle for almost 20 years.

Now back to my son who is physically no more.

I came home that Friday and cried that whole weekend with my family and Shamika. On Sunday we went to her father's house to get ready for the funeral on Monday. I didn't sleep much that night. I was up early the next morning trying to pray and find some peace and strength for what was coming in a few hours.

The funeral was at the Inglewood cemetery, across the street from the Forum where the Lakers used to play. I invited Lil Man. My boy who picked me up from jail came with his kids and their mother. A lot of my family came. So did Shamika's family. My father did the eulogy. Before the funeral began, we had a viewing of the body.

I'll never forget baby Oscar's face. He had a frown on his face and his body was hard like a plastic doll. I couldn't contain myself at all. Neither could my mother. That day was so difficult for me. Only by God's grace and I am alive today because I thought about killing myself a lot that day.

If you're not living right with God and you lose your only child let this be a warning to all. Pray and repent so one day you will be with your child again.

My father did a great job at the funeral. He is definitely a strong man because I was lost in a daze of misery and guilt.

Shamika made sure baby Oscar's favorite song was playing in the background, *The Sweetest Thing*, by Lauryn Hill.

Even as I write these memories down, it's a little difficult for me to express every detail properly.

After my father did the eulogy, we went to the other side of the mortuary to put baby Oscar in the ground or to "rest" as they call it. I read a poem I wrote for him and put it on top of his coffin. What a birthday. I turned 22 years old and was burying my son.

I rode with Lil Man back to my parents' house so I could smoke some marijuana. No one in my family did drugs. I needed to escape from the pain so I chose drugs instead of God. This was also the first day I used cocaine. But it definitely wouldn't be my last.

I have a problem picking friends in my life so far. I try to find the good in people. I try to develop a family with them as well. This hasn't really worked out well for me because I wasn't mentally capable or spiritually prepared to build anything solid with anyone.

I really hope I don't lose anyone's attention as they read this story. This is a lot more difficult than expected yet extremely gratifying as well. I can feel the weight of all these years and the bad decisions being lifted off my shoulders.

Before I get back to the death of my son, I just want to take a break and share with you my feelings today.

My father is such an amazing man. He sent me a Father's Day card a couple of days ago. Even though it was late, the message was beautiful. He's the only person who sent me anything for Father's Day. I'm fighting back tears as I write this partly because I'm in the TV room around a bunch of inmates and this particular group is pretty judgmental.

The card my father sent me says:

To a new Dad on Father's Day

You dreamed of how wonderful life would be as a new Dad and wished for it all to come true. May it be everything you hoped for and even more amazing, too!

That was the actual message on the card but my Dad's message went just like this:

To a new Dad, a new person in Christ, to a new man and Child of God. It is this Dad's hope that this is your last time in jail or prison. Our family needs every one of us for many reasons. But we have to be present and accounted for if we hope to make a positive influence in the lives of those we care about. All of your children as well as to religious guidance, protection, security, hope and the other necessities of life, so we must put ourselves in a position of sacrifice to help make their lives better. God is good and He will make a way where there seems not to be a way. We must be willing to take His way. A beautiful example of this is found in the story of the Prodigal Son. When life gets tough, and it will; when it seems like nothing is going your way and it will; when you seem as though you are all alone and it will; Know God!

These beautiful words were enclosed in the Father's Day card my daddy sent to me. My father has been encouraging me like this since I've been in jail and even before. He's a great man, flaws and all, but truly great. He has given me a lot of godly direction in life. I didn't always listen but I totally get it now.

OK, so back to baby Oscar.

I drove to my parent's house with Lil Man and got really high. As we approached the house, I noticed balloons and realized it was my birthday. Instead of being happy and thankful, I was angry and very uncomfortable, partly because I was under the influence. I still went along with it and accepted the gifts and enjoyed my family and Shamika's company.

I had a few more days of freedom before I had to turn myself back into the WVDC jail in San Bernardino. I spent most of that time with Shamika and family and friends.

The night before I turned myself in Shamika and I talked about our future. We made plans to be together and rebuild our relationship. I didn't sleep much that night. I let my mind wander instead of talking to God like I do now.

Shamika and I got up early and got dressed. She drove me to the courthouse. It was still early so we cuddled in the backseat and shared another intimate moment before court. Shamika and I were very emotional. Neither one of us wanted to say goodbye. We went into the courtroom. The judge called my name and I was remanded back into custody. This was Friday, March 17th, 2000. My actual release date was at the end of April.

I still had the probation hold from Los Angeles so I wasn't going to be free in April. But I will be free soon. I was sure of that.

After my time was done, Los Angeles came to pick me up. I was processed into the Men's Central Jail in downtown LA. I spent a couple of months on Denver row then I was transferred to Wayside County Jail near Magic Mountain.

When I got to the jail another riot happened between the Blacks and Hispanics. They had to keep us all separated. My court date was coming soon, but not soon enough.

While I was in this jail, I was housed in the supermax section. I reconnected with a friend I met through one of my best friends, a rapper named Dirty Rat. His name was JC and he was a DJ fighting a murder case. He was very distant and didn't have much to say to me. I also met a good friend from Pasadena named Kyrie Dosier aka KD.

The way we met was very ironic. We were in separate dorms and for some reason, we were showing pictures. He showed me his girl named Charmaine. She was a Filipino girl I met through a girl I used to date named Silvia. My friend Lil Man ended up taking Silvia from me and one of our mutual friends Red had dated Charmaine. I told KD about it and we just got close from there.

The tension in this jail was very strong. All I wanted to do was go home. But before my court date, I suffered more pain.

Shamika and I would talk often on the phone and she came to visit me a few times. But one day I kept calling her and I couldn't get through to her. I eventually called her cousin's house. I was told Shamika had been at some guy's house since the night before. I instantly got sad. I shed a few tears because I knew in my heart, she was sleeping with him.

I eventually got a hold of Shamika and confronted her like a man and told her to be honest with me. She decided to tell me the truth. I was right. She had slept with him. She said she felt horrible about it and that it wouldn't happen again.

See, Shamika was living at my parent's house, waiting for me to come home. But sometimes she would go to Compton to stay with her aunt.

I forgave her. I was released a week later.

One of the many things I've learned about going to jail is you will get left most of the time by the one you may have called your soulmate. It takes a very strong person to stand behind you when you are incarcerated. It also takes a godly connection to have true love.

As strong as I've been in my present state of mind, it still hurts a little when I think about how many times I've been abandoned by the one I loved at the time of each incarceration. Especially this time, while in federal custody. I put a lot into this girl. I even tattooed her name on the top of my chest.

Cristal. That's her name. But we aren't together anymore.

As good as I was to her, I was also bad. I told lies, I cheated, I put her down at times. She was equally offensive to me. Regardless, two wrongs don't make a right. I have a lot to say about her. I'll save it for the end of the story- where she belongs.

Thanks to her, I finally know how to love a woman again. I also have learned a lot about myself and what I deserve in a relationship. Most importantly, I'm closer to God than I've ever been.

I've always liked to write my thoughts on paper in the form of a story, poetry, and music. I got really good at it right before baby Oscar died. When I finally got released from jail I was driven to record as much music as I could and to build relationships with people in the industry.

Shamika and I tried to make it work but the love diminished between us.

Then tragedy struck again.

One of my good friends I met through Brian named Wayne was killed in a tragic accident on the 14 freeway, headed to Slush's house. It was September 9th, 2000. His birthday. He was 28 years old.

Even though Wayne and I were friends before he went to jail, we really started to get closer when I got out. I would share songs I wrote or recorded with him. He would give his honest opinion on what he thought of them. Most of the time he liked what I was doing and a couple of times he would share his ideas for songs as well. Now he is gone just like that. One day we were sharing music and the next day he was dead.

I went to the wake to view the body. I didn't go to the funeral. It was just too much for me to handle after dealing with the loss of my son.

I started doing drugs a little more. Shamika and I were almost completely done and I started sleeping with a lot of women. One of these women was a pretty Italian girl named Nichole I met in Long Beach while visiting another woman. I was living life recklessly, but at the time, everything seemed normal to me. I slept with Nichole a few times but we never took it further than that.

Then I met this girl from Detroit who wanted to move to Los Angeles to pursue her dreams. It's sad I don't remember her name but her name doesn't matter as much as her purpose does in my life then. She had good credit and money saved to get an apartment so we decided to move in together. It was a very nice apartment on Sepulveda right by LAX. Right before we moved in on Friday, October 13th, 2000 another tragedy hit me like a ton of bricks.

Out of nowhere, my grandmother on my mom's side passed away due to complications with cancer. This took my depression to a whole new level and depleted my faith. I said a lot of foul words to God at that time. I was crushed by the deaths of my son, my friend and now, my grandma.

She was the last one I had left. All of my grandparents had already passed but this was the worst. She and I were very close. Everyone in my family went except me. I was a total mess. I didn't know what to do. My bitterness caused me to create multiple personalities to help me live every day like nothing happened.

No sooner than the girl from Detroit and I moved in together, she decided to move out because I was no good for her. I took her for granted and cheated on her openly.

By this time, I was heavily connected to the music business. I was working with mega producer Michaelangelo Saulsberry, Fred Crawford of Launch Pad, Madd Funk, Wu Tang, Dame Lee, 3rd Storee, Teddy Riley, Damian and Aaron Hall, Mad Lux, Ray J, Young Buck, Les "Law" Whitaker (who was living with me at the time) and many more. I had a manager named Lewis Taylor.

I was still doing bank fraud. I was never broke, and I was living like a king. My ego was out of control but I still had a soft spot for love. My heart wanted to be in a real relationship. My body wanted a new girl every day. I wasn't rooted in the Word of God at all then. For the most part, I gave up on God and replaced Him with sex, drugs, and rock and roll.

I was a very vulgar person. What's strange is I rarely used cuss words in my music besides the "N" word- which was OK with me at that time. I didn't know it then but now I can see how God always kept His eyes on me and his hands on my heart, slowly drawing me back to him.

In the midst of my musical adventures, I went to the big Hollywood clubs often. One particular night I went to the Key Club on Sunset for a special event. As soon as I walked in I ran into three women I used to have crushes on: Maritza, Cora, and Michaelia.

I met each girl at different stages in my life and now they were all very close friends. Maritza and Michaelia were actually in a group together. For some reason, Michaelia and I couldn't keep our hands off each other. I told her I had my own place and wanted her to come spend the night. We exchanged numbers and said our goodbyes. I went straight home and made preparations for her to come over.

She called me at about 2 or 3 am and I directed her to my house. She was driving a white Nissan Altima. I was so excited to finally have her this close to me. I even talked to her on the phone and waited outside her building until she pulled up.

Companionship is a wonderful thing, I must admit, but I placed too much faith in love. I never understood until now.

Michaelia was very beautiful, half Filipino and African American. She had a young son around 4 years old. Michaelia and I were the same sign. Both of our birthdays were in early March. We just had this chemistry that was electric. Our first night together was full of passion, desire, and affection. Even though I had an arsenal of women, I instantly wanted to make her the one.

Our relationship grew rapidly. We spent a lot of time together for the first couple of months in a very happy place. Her son and I became close almost as fast as she and I did. He eventually started calling me Dad. I was happy to accept this title since I was still grieving over the loss of baby Oscar. Most of my friends quickly became cool with Michaelia. We recorded a lot of music together and really enjoyed each other's company. I spent so much time focused on her, that I started forgetting my responsibilities.

Michaelia was also from Long Beach. Her father, a military vet, lived there. Her mother lived in Seattle. Michaelia had a trip planned to see her mother and her kid brother. I was so attached to her that I didn't want her to go. But of course, that didn't stop her, so I took her to the airport.

As she was about to check into her flight, I grabbed her hand, got down on one knee, and asked her to be my wife. I really thought she was the one and I was confident in our connection. She said yes. We kissed and said our goodbyes. I watched the plane take off, a very happy man. She was only gone a week but it seemed like a lot longer.

As I write these memories, I'm amazed at how clear some of my life experiences are to me. That's why I have to admit all drugs are bad for you. Especially marijuana. It makes you forget and suppress things you need to release and let go. Most of my adult life experiences have hindered me from progressing. I'm just so thankful to be clear-minded and aware.

I got evicted from my place and had to move in with Michaelia. She lived in an apartment in Bellflower around the corner from my parents' home. One of my boys who was living with me came to stay with us as well. This is where our relationship started going downhill.

We started arguing about money and she started treating me like I was nothing to her. Her son and I had built such a strong bond it kept us together. My mother didn't trust her or care for her that much. She just had a very uncomfortable feeling about her. Around this time my mother had found a civil attorney out of Irvine to file a medical malpractice suit against Antelope Valley Hospital and the doctor who administered baby Oscar the wrong medicine.

Michaelia and I would break up and get back together all the time, mainly because her son missed me and would ask for me often. That little boy was a very special child. I still think of him today.

A couple of years passed by and she and I were still together. She had done some pretty cruel things to me. I was too blind to see it for what it was.

After moving a couple of times we eventually got a place in Van Nuys. We rented a room with one of my friends who had a townhouse. I was working with Mad House Entertainment and recording music with Mark Sparx and Kevin Backstrom of Soul Life, Beat Brokerz and G-Hop music.

I was also getting close to settling my lawsuit. I thought it would bring me a large amount of money. I trusted too many people with too much information. I was really blind to things that are very clear to me now.

I was spending a lot of time with my best friend Chris Reese aka Dirty Rat doing music with him at his new company, Stiffarm Entertainment. Dirty Rat had recently left Loud Records and was going the independent route. J.C. was still his DJ then as well as after beating that murder case in 2000 or 2001. I was also doing a lot of dirt with Lil Man and a couple of my friends who gangbanged. My drug intake continued to grow. I had no control over it or myself. I really only have one reason for my survival and that's God above. He obviously had a plan for my life that exceeded any of my expectations.

I had too many people in my life and I called too many of them friends and family. I really had issues but I also still had Michaelia. Michaelia and I had a strong physical connection. We also did a lot as a family. Her son and I continued to get closer and closer to the point where I loved him and considered him my own. This connection made me want children with Michaelia but due to my inconsistent income, she didn't feel the same. She became pregnant twice. Both times, she decided to get abortions against my wishes. I didn't find out about one of the abortions until our relationship was almost over. Michaelia was a totally different breed of woman than I was used to and I couldn't let her go. Our relationship became toxic and, at times, abusive on both ends.

By now it was 2002 and I was close to settling the lawsuit for baby Oscar's death. I thought I was going to receive a large settlement but apparently, there is a cap of $250,000 for a malpractice lawsuit for a child 6 years old and under. They call it non-economic loss. When my attorney informed my mother and me about this, I was devastated.

To make matters worse, a private investigator was hired to track down Shamika so she could get part of the settlement. Shamika and I weren't speaking and she wasn't even involved in any part of the lawsuit. Eventually, they found her and set up a meeting between us and the doctor who killed my son so we could negotiate a settlement. My lawyer said he would try to get as close to the 250k cap as possible. We came to an agreement of 190k. I wasn't happy about this, but my attorney advised us to take it. Then everything got really interesting.

Shamika decided she wanted a bigger percentage than me because I was in jail when he died. She said she wouldn't sign off on the case unless I agreed to a 60/40 split. I couldn't believe this was happening especially after all my mother and father did for all of us. This was a big blow to our plans.

We went back and forth and finally agreed to a 59/51 split, the lesser end being mine. My attorney's fee was 33%. So, at the end of the day, I received 44k for the death of my son.

I could spend so much time telling you the long end of this part of my story but I have so much to tell you and I want to save myself the embarrassment. I squandered the money on drugs, friends, Michaelia, a Lexus and I put out an album.

I realize now that part of the reason Michaelia stuck around was because of the settlement. The truth hurts and can be embarrassing, but it's still the truth. After the money was gone, Michaelia and I were back at each other's throats arguing over money and other things.

I started doing check fraud again with my boys. We took it to Vegas and a few other states. After having a larger taste for money, I started taking more risks.

While in Vegas, my boy Goldie and I met some girls from Milwaukee, Wisconsin. They had been stranded in Vegas by some crazy guys they met in LA. They were both extremely beautiful so we decided to assist in any way we could to repair the damage of their first trip to Vegas. We got a hotel room on the strip and treated them like queens.

I was still with Michaelia but she was doing a lot of things behind my back. So I decided to create a double life as well.

Both of these girls became very close to me and Goldie. We finished our business in Vegas and went back to California. One of the girls had to fly back home to Wisconsin for school. But the one I was with was living in a rented house in Pasadena with friends. She and I became very close and we actually liked each other. I decided to stay with her for a few days. I made up a lie and told Michaelia I was on a money mission, which was only half of the story. I was using my charm to get this girl to fully trust me.

It took me no time and within a week I sent a check to her little sister for 5k. She cashed it and sent me a little over 4k through Western Union. I gave this girl a little money, gave Goldie his cut and I kept the rest.

I was also in consistent communication with her friend who was in college from Wisconsin. Her friend and I decided it would be a good idea for me to fly to Milwaukee, introduce this scam to her friends and get paid. I gave Michaelia some money and told her I was going to Milwaukee with my boys to hustle. But in actuality, I was going by myself to stay with this girl and scam all of her friends.

I was so driven by financial possibilities I didn't think anything could go wrong. I told Goldie my plans and of course, he was with it in every way. I bought my ticket at the airport and caught the next plane to Milwaukee.

I had never been to the midwest and I was excited by this adventure I had conjured up. I felt invincible. I also felt like I was protected by God's grace. I didn't have a clear understanding of being double-minded. I truly believed I had God's blessing in my illegal scheme of money-making.

The flight was pretty quick and I was picked up by one of the girls I met in Vegas. This particular girl was a lot more intelligent than her friend in Pasadena. We instantly turned into more than friends. We were intimate with each other that night and the next day she showed me the city.

She lived off-campus in an apartment with a roommate. I used her computer to set up the programs I used to create business checks. I had her call a few of her friends and ask them if they wanted to make some big, fast, money. A few of her friends said yes instantly and we were off to the races.

We dropped off checks to a few different girls and gave them instructions on how to deposit them. I told them how much I wanted from each transaction. That afternoon we went to the mall and I met some more people.

While she was in a lady's store, I saw this beautiful blond haired, blue eyed young lady working at a cell phone kiosk. I approached her flirtatiously and we hit it off instantly. We exchanged numbers and I told her I would be calling her soon. There was something very special about this girl. Oh, and her name was Jessica. Actually, her full name was Jessica Lee Holm. I'll explain later about why I remembered her full name.

Later that evening, my college connection took me out to a bar and we got pretty drunk. She was actually the drunk one. I was slightly buzzed. I've never been a heavy drinker. After the bar, we went back to her place and ended our evening sexually, of course.

While she slept, I called Jessica. We talked about different things like future plans and goals in life. We also made plans to see each other the next day. I went to sleep feeling very confident in my current position.

That morning I called Michaelia and told her I was about to get super paid and that we would do something really special for her upcoming birthday in a few days. After that, we got a few calls from her friends to pick up our funds. I call these events the "white envelope moment."

I believe we picked up a little over 10k by 1 PM that day. I gave the baby girl a nice piece of change and I pocketed $8,500 for myself. We went to the mall again and ran a few other errands. I told her all about Jessica and our plans for that evening. She had no problem with my decision, especially since I just paid her rent for the next 3 months. We were intimate again, then I took a shower and got ready for my date with Jessica.

Jessica picked me up at about 6 PM in a blue Honda Accord. She was dressed in some tight jeans and a designer top, her hair hanging below her shoulders. This woman was even more beautiful than I remembered. We went to dinner then she took me back to her place.

We talked about her family and finishing college and about my music and family as well. Our chemistry was very electric and I felt comfortable with her. We decided to watch a movie and she made herself more comfortable. I remember the white sweats she wore like it was yesterday. I believe they were from Victoria's Secret. We lay on her couch and cuddled very closely. One thing led to another and we were skin-to-skin. We couldn't keep our hands off of each other that entire night. We slept like babies and I remember never thinking about Michaelia at all.

Jessica reminded me of my relationship with Debra and Sheila. They were all intelligent and focused on a productive life. The next morning, I didn't want to leave her but I had to go pick up more money and make a few drops. I was so excited about Jessica; that I didn't think much about anything else.

Little did I know my life was about to take another drastic turn for the worse.

After Jessica dropped me off, I immediately started getting everything together for my money-making mission. My Milwaukee connection was still in bed, sick and hungover from the night before. She told me two of her friends kept calling her wanting to talk to me about more checks. I didn't think anything of it. I told them to come to her place and pick them up. What a mistake that was.

When they finally came to pick them up, I noticed an edgy vibe about them. I blew it off and gave them their checks.

As I went into the apartment, I noticed a couple of police cars but didn't think much of it. After counting some more money and preparing some more checks there was a loud knock on the door. The girl I was with asked me to answer. When

I looked through the window, I saw the police. I instantly ran to the back door and tried to escape but the place was surrounded. They immediately arrested me and searched the place for evidence.

They searched and talked to the girl I was with. She obviously cooperated with them because she wasn't arrested. They took me to jail, booked me, and charged me with check fraud. Apparently, the girls had set me up. I didn't cover my tracks well enough and got caught.

I called my mother first who was very upset but understanding as well. Then I called Michaelia who was pretty upset as well. Her birthday was the next day and I wasn't going to be there. I had somehow managed to remember Jessica's number. When I called her, she was very understanding and came to visit me. I didn't know anyone else in Milwaukee but her.

As bad as I was, God still provided for me. Jessica wrote me letters and visited me a few times. Michaelia wrote to me maybe twice and pretty much told me she was moving on without actually saying those words. Her actions spoke very loud to me.

After a few months in downtown Milwaukee, I was transferred to the House of Corrections a couple of hours outside Milwaukee. I went to court a few times for my preliminary hearing and a few other court proceedings. I was guilty and just hoping for a good deal.

Jessica and I became close through all of this and made plans to be together when I got out. I got along with most of the men I was incarcerated with. I also tried to restore my faith in God by attending church and Bible studies. I wrote a lot of music and poetry and finally found my voice as a rap artist. I developed my own style and became pretty good at it. Other inmates would hear me and word spread around the jail fast.

A couple of months before I got arrested a few friends and I performed at the Apollo Theater in Harlem, New York. We actually did well and didn't get booed off stage. As I recall we were the first rap group to not get kicked off the stage.

One evening, while I was locked up in the House of Corrections, this particular episode of Showtime at the Apollo came on television. The entire jail watched the show faithfully. While my dorm was watching, I realized this was the episode I was on. I made a few friends while I was there. I got really excited and told them. One of them, Jacquincy, who was like a brother to me, and the other one named James, heard my excitement and came to the television area.

After my group's performance, the whole dorm, including the corrections officers, looked at me differently. Most of them couldn't understand why I was in jail when I had so much talent. I actually said the same thing to myself, but unlike them, I had the answer.

I didn't have my priorities in order. I didn't put God first. I know better now but at that time I still believed in fast money and women. I served these desires over my faith in God. For some people that lifestyle works for them but when God has a plan for your life nothing you do will work until you put Him first. You will see more about my calling after you see how many times I got blessed even though I was guilty of the crimes I committed.

Days turned into weeks, weeks into months and one day my attorney came to visit me. He said the prosecutor wanted me to sign a plea for 0 to 4 years in jail. This was called an open plea. He advised me that if I went to trial I would get a lot more time. With this in mind, I decided to sign the plea agreement. Before he left, he said we would be in court in a few days to accept the plea and be sentenced.

I called my mother and father and told them what happened. Even though my parents were very upset, they maintained a positive state of mind and prayed for me. I also called my real father's mother, my Grandma Augustine.

She and I started talking a year or so ago before I went to jail. It was a relief because I had lost all of my other grandparents. So, it was a blessing to have her in my life. I was telling her what my attorney had said when she interrupted me, asking if I would like to speak to someone. I wasn't sure who would want to talk to me so I asked who it was.

She said, "Your dad is here and he would like to talk to you."

As nervous as I was, I was also eager to hear his voice. I said, "Put him on please, Grandma."

When my biological father got on the phone, I could tell he was slightly under the influence of alcohol. We said hello and he told me a few stories about my mother. He had a lot of excuses as to why he stayed out of my life. He blamed it on my mother and father. He said my dad "stole" me from him. It didn't make sense to me, but I listened anyway. Our conversation did nothing for me except make me feel sorry for him. We said goodbye and I continued my conversation with Grandma Augustine.

At that time, my Grandfather Oscar was still alive, but he was sick, battling cancer. Still, my grandparents were always happy to talk to me. As happy as I was with having living grandparents, I still struggled with receiving the blessing of having them.

I got off the phone with them, called Jessica and told her what happened with my attorney visit. She said she would be there for me and that she loved me. As I think of her, I wish I wasn't so jaded by all the women who left and hurt me before her. This was unfair to her. She was a great woman who had her life in order. I was too blind to see her worth or accept her properly.

Michaelia still had my heart even though she broke it repeatedly. I even wrote poetry and songs about her. I tried calling her to tell her what happened but I couldn't get her to answer my calls. She had moved on, married a man named Jason, and was pregnant with their first child. I didn't find this out until a few months later. But that's a story within itself.

Now back to my upcoming sentence date. Even though I knew Jesus and attended Bible studies, I didn't have both feet rooted in His Word and principles, but God still took care of me for some reason. The night before my sentencing date, the Christian brothers prayed with me and laid hands on me.

I don't remember sleeping that much that night but I remember begging and pleading with God for mercy. I had been locked up for a little over 10 months- my longest stretch in jail besides the 8½ months I did in San Bernardino.

The corrections officers woke me up at 4:30 that morning. I ate a quick breakfast and got shackled around my ankles and waist. There weren't many of us going to court that day.

The officers called each of our names and directed us to get on the bus after our name had been called.

The bus ride was quiet and the temperature was pretty cold, being wintertime. I remember my whole life flashing through my mind like a movie. Before I could really gather all of my thoughts, we arrived at the courthouse. The COs unloaded us off the bus and led us to a holding cell. They took off our restraints and locked us in the cell. It was 7 am and my court date wasn't until 9:30.

At about 9 am, my attorney came down to see me. We went over the plea agreement and I had to sign a few papers. I was also informed that my mother and father were in the courtroom. I was shocked and filled with disbelief that my parents would fly to Milwaukee, Wisconsin to witness me being sentenced. I was filled with guilt and embarrassment, but there was also a touch of happiness and joy.

After I collected my thoughts, I asked my attorney if he was sure that my parents were really there. He confirmed it by describing my beautiful mother and handsome father. I finished signing off all of the paperwork. I was handcuffed and escorted to the courtroom. Sure enough, I saw both of my parents with very sad looks on their faces.

To be sitting in prison again writing this story about my life and remembering all that I put my family through eats away at my soul. I can never allow greed and my selfish ways to pull me away from a family who actually loves me. As much as they have hurt me, I believe I've gone way beyond them by all of my criminal actions. Even though my crimes didn't affect them, they definitely did indirectly.

Chapter 4

As I think about that court date in Milwaukee, I can see the extreme sadness and disappointment on both of their faces. I remember smiling when I saw them. They actually managed to crack a smile behind all that sadness and my heart couldn't take it. Tears flowed down my eyes and guilt swept through me like a hurricane.

I approached the bench. The judge asked me my name and read my charges. Before announcing my sentence, he asked me to speak. I spoke about my family and my dreams and goals. I apologized to the court for my criminal acts.

After I spoke, the judge spoke candidly to me. He gave me compliments and praised my parents, whom he met in the hall earlier as he came to work.

Then he said if he met me in the free world, he could see us being friends.

My attorney and the prosecutor were surprised by those comments.

Then the judge asked my parents to speak. My mother tried to, but she couldn't get the words out without crying. My father managed to get his point across articulately, although he had some tears in his eyes.

After the judge heard my parents speak, he said, "I sentence you to four years. Here are the terms. One year in jail and three years' supervised release." He told me that after this, he wanted me to get out of jail and get my life in order.

I instantly thanked God and I thanked him for this merciful sentence. My parents were very happy. So was my attorney. This meant I had less than two months of jail time left. This also meant I was still going to prison even though it would be a short trip.

After court, I was transported back to the H.O.C. The ride back felt comfortable and peaceful due to this weight taken off my shoulders. When I got back to my unit, I shared the news with my friends as well as my Christian brothers.

Friendship means more to me today than it ever did in my entire life. The reason being, due to all the friends I've acquired in my lifetime. Even though the title was friend, now, after I've evaluated each relationship, most of them were only acquaintances. I have no anger or resentment towards any of them. I don't wish to continue being friends or acquaintances with a large number of them. I choose now to have friends who are believers in God and who follow some, if not all, of the principles I follow.

As I continue to share my life experience with you readers, I will also drift away continually and share my thoughts and perspectives on the events I write about and my current state of mind in the summer of 2016.

My apologies to you if this slightly annoys you but I really hope you bear with me and stay the course as I share my life with you.

OK. Back to the House of Corrections.

After receiving my sentence, it took me about a week to get shipped off to prison. This would be my very first time in the prison system and I was scared. The place I was headed to was called Dodge Prison, about four hours away from Milwaukee. I've heard so many different prison stories and seen my share of prison movies. My nerves were all over the place. But you know what? After I got to Dodge, I realized jail was jail and I actually like prison better than the county jail.

*I will never say I enjoy being in jail **ever**.* I love freedom but compared to county jail, prison is much better. There are more things to do, better food, and more respect among inmates. My time at Dodge was so short. I barely remember a thing about the place.

After Dodge, I was released to a halfway house in Milwaukee and assigned to a parole officer. I don't remember her name, but I do remember her being super cool. She knew I wanted to go back to California, so she began doing a transfer for me called an interstate agreement. In this agreement, Los Angeles County would either accept me back or deny me into their society.

You had to have a solid address and family, as well as a plan set-up for employment.

After I met with my PO and got set-up in the halfway house, Jessica came to see me. We instantly started spending a lot of time together and making plans for the future but my heart was so twisted.

Due to all the pain of being left by other women, I started developing multiple personalities and relationships with other women. Even though Jessica was my girl I still had other women, which came so easy for me. Within 2 weeks of my release, I had 5 or 6 other girlfriends who were really into me. This is when I turned a gift into a curse and became a brutal player. Jessica had no idea what I had become. I really became a compulsive liar and no one could tell. I was so good at deception and manipulation.

Before I continue with my spring 2004 section of my life journey, I have to share with you a passage of scripture. It's from the book of Ephesians 4:25-32.

> *25 Therefore each of you must put off falsehood and speak truthfully to your neighbor, for we are all members of one body.26 "In your anger do not sin"[d]: Do not let the sun go down while you are still angry,27 and do not give the devil a foothold.28 Anyone who has been stealing must steal no longer but must work, doing something useful with their own hands, so that they may have something to share with those in need.29 Do not let any unwholesome talk come out of your mouths, but only what is helpful for building others up according to their needs, that it may benefit those who listen.30 And do not grieve the Holy Spirit of God, with whom you were sealed for the day of redemption.31 Get rid of all bitterness, rage and anger, brawling and slander, along with every form of malice.32 Be kind and compassionate to*

one another, forgiving each other, just as in Christ
God forgave you.

Once a day, usually in the evening, I read a book in the Bible. I do this exercise for a whole month then I switch to another book at the beginning of next month. I also do a special reading every morning around 9 or 10 am. I've learned in these past two years that in order to live a godly lifestyle, I must know, practice and memorize the Word of God.

The apostle Paul called for all believers to speak the truth to each other because all believers are united in Christ. Paul instructed us not to allow anger to fester or continue for long. Christians may respond in controlled anger to injustice and sin, but they should never be consumed by this anger. Instead, they should seek opportunities to express Christ's love to everyone. We are also called to share with the needy and to allow corrupt words to come out of our mouths because the standard of speech for Christians is very high. The Holy Spirit of God should never be pushed away, ignored, or rejected.

As you see, I was then and up until December of 2014 living a double-minded lifestyle. I was a believer in God and an employee of the devil. The wrath of God was heavy on me and light at the same time. The heavy side shows in all the times I went to jail. The light side is his consistent mercy on me when it comes to the time, I spent in jail each time up until now. I don't tell you this to scare you or preach to you. I tell you this to make you aware in case you're living the way I was living. If you're still living like that, please stop before it's too late and you ruin your heavenly status. As long as you're alive, heaven is an option. All you have to do is believe and receive Jesus as your Lord and Savior.

Now back to Milwaukee.

It's very humbling and sad to think of how many opportunities I've allowed to pass by me between baby Oscar and Jessica. Not to brag, but I was friends with Mark Wahlberg briefly, due to my deeper friendship with his brother, Johnny. I used to hang out at Mark's house on Doheny Drive in Beverly Hills and with Jamie Foxx on Vanalden in the valley.

Did music with so many legends. Stayed at Marvin Gaye's house and was signed to his son, Marvin Gaye Jr who had a label called M3 Records. I built bridges with Ron Devoe of New Edition and Michaelangelo of Portrait. Had a bond with Ray J and Brandy Norwood through my close friends Shorty Mac and Sean Young. Connected with Static Major of the group Playa and Aaliyah and Rodney "Darkchild" Jenkins.

Was a longtime member of the Chrystal Cathedral Ministries pastored by the legendary Robert Schullar. Rubbed elbows with Maya Angelou, Norman Vincent Peale, Armond Hammer, Stephanie Mills, Chaka Khan, Bobby Brown, Tevin Campbell, Angela Windbush, and Norman Whitfield.

I could go on and on but here I was in the Midwest fresh out of prison, creating more lies and missing a lot of teeth due to a gum disease that was destroying my teeth. Basically, I was cursed and I could only blame myself. God gave me so many opportunities. I was too blind to see them and too arrogant to appreciate them.

After two months at the halfway house, I was allowed to move in with Jessica until my transfer was complete. Jessica lived in a nice apartment on Lisbon Ave that her family owned. As much as I thought I loved Jessica, I couldn't allow myself to be vulnerable like I had been before her. Regardless, she was there for me and treated me the way a man should be treated. But I wasn't satisfied with that. I wanted to be a rap star and actor. That was my mission.

After a few weeks of living with Jessica, my transfer was approved. I was definitely a lot more excited than she was. Even though she wanted me to stay in Milwaukee, she also wanted me to pursue my dreams and be close to my family. We made plans to make it work long distance and it was off to the airport for me.

My parole office in Milwaukee was able to get me transferred to the parole building in Long Beach off the 405 Cherry St exit. This was perfect. My family lived in Bellflower so the commute would be quick and easy. My orders were to report to my new parole officer Mr. Barnes within 24 hours of my arrival in Los Angeles. The flight was quick. My family picked me up from the airport. They were happy to see me which was very comforting.

While I was in jail, my family had moved from Eucalyptus Ave to a house across the street from the high school I graduated from. This was a very nice adjustment but not much room for me. I was bound for the couch but that was OK. I had plans to connect with many of my industry friends and crash with them.

Every word in this story is true. I'm not bragging or name dropping. This is just the world I created for myself. Between 2004 to 2010, this is my circle of friends and acquaintances. Adam Brown aka AB (singer/ songwriter), Chris Reece aka Dirty Rat (rapper/actor), Justin Marshall aka JuJu (industry executive), Zane Copeland aka Lil Zane (rapper/actor), Al Benet (music producer/engineer), Berry Reed aka Jay R (singer/songwriter), Lamont Bentley (actor), Jonathon McDaniel aka Lil J (actor/rapper), Sean Young (actor/producer), Desmond Mapp aka Big Dez (artist/producer), Ciarra Carter (actress), John Schuller aka JC, Sean Kingston (singer/ rapper), CJ Hilton (singer/producer), Omar Gooding (actor), Salim Grant (actor/singer), Crystal Grant (actor/singer), Ziggy Jackson (rapper), Jackie Jackson (industry executive, part of the Jackson 5), Brandon Howard (singer/producer), Deja (producer/executive), Tiffany Sayer (singer/ writer), Pauly Paul (producer/executive), Pete Farmer (executive), Darrell Owens aka Shorty Mac (actor rapper), Amber Hopson aka Cobra Red (rapper/hair stylist), Mike Williams (engineer, musician), Dawn Monique Scruggs (singer/writer), Megan Good (actress), Brandon T Jackson (actor/ comedian), Demario aka Raz B of B2K (artist/actor), Ricky Romance (executive and Raz's brother), Damio (son of Chaka Khan) and many more.

The reason I did a layout of each of these names and professions is because they all played a part in my personal life and my growth as an artist. As I began to share my love life between these 6 years many of these individuals were a part of many of these changes. I'm actually still friends with many of these talented people to this day but I'm a totally different man now so we will see how they react to the new me.

Now let's get back to 2004.

My first visit with my parole officer went pretty well. He gave me instructions, advised me to follow my dreams and stay away from the criminal aspect of things. Of course, I said OK, but I was already back to many of my old habits.

I thought this way of thinking was OK as long as I had a positive ending. But truthfully speaking, when God has a plan for your life, your best bet is to seek Him. Listen to His voice and follow His teachings or things will never be joy filled in your life no matter how much money and success you achieve. At this time, I was still trying to use God for my benefit only.

I started reconnecting with Ab, Dirty Rat and JuJu. Ab had a million-dollar deal with the Foster brothers and JuJu was his right-hand man. Dirty Rat was about to put out an independent album through his own label. He was my best friend and he believed in me musically. They all lived in the valley so that's pretty much where I spent most of my time. JuJu dealt with a lot of producers so he started giving me beats to write to and Ab allowed me to stay with them pretty often. Ab had just done a record with a pretty well-known rapper, Lil Zane featuring another well- known singer, Tank. Ab was so talented. He has a voice crispier than Maxwell and he was Hispanic. We were friends before I went to prison so he accepted me back into his life like I never left.

AB and JuJu were best friends and roommates. We all got along well. JuJu was a ladies man like me so he immediately connected me with various women. One woman who caught me instantly was an exotic dancer named Iris. She worked at a strip club with JuJu's girlfriend, Erica. She was a beautiful Mexican girl with a perfect shape, amazing smile and very laid-back attitude. Erica told her a lot about me and one night our paths crossed perfectly. We exchanged numbers and made plans to see each other soon.

A couple of days later I was staying the night at JuJu and Ab's house. I asked Erica to persuade Iris to come back with her after work. Apparently, Iris was a lot more interested in me then I thought because that evening, she stopped by and we became inseparable. I was still communicating with Jessica but Iris quickly had my full attention.

That morning, I went home with Iris and we became a couple. JuJu and Erica weren't surprised because they both knew me and my abilities with women very well. Iris had a ML 500 Mercedes truck and I drove it often. I would take her to work at the strip club then I would go about my day.

At this time, I had also reconnected with my close friend Jay R who was a singer in this group called 3rd Storee. The label housed them in a celebrity-filled apartment complex called the Archstone in Studio City. Jay R's neighbors were Kanye West, Keisha Cole, Eva Mendez and many more. So of course, I spent a lot of time at this complex due to the networking environment. I also spent a lot of time here because Jay R and I were close like brothers and I was also friends with his group members. Jay R had a gift with music and we started recording a lot of music together.

Sometimes we would have so many musical ideas I would bring him home to the apartment I shared with Iris in Canyon Country.

Iris had a son and we got along wonderfully. Even though I still talked to Jessica, I considered myself faithful to Iris. Of course, I know better now that my mind is clear and drug free and also because I love the Lord. But at this time for me and my twisted soul, I was a one- woman man. This was only the beginning of these temporary love spells. After a few months, Iris and I started to grow apart.

I won't use this book to slander people and blame them for my downfalls. I will just reveal mostly what I did unless the parties involved did something to me that must be exposed. Towards the end of Iris and I many factors came into play, some bigger than others.

It was shortly after Christmas of 2004 that one of my friends, Dermaine, from my group Cavey Express told me in a casual conversation over some marijuana that I had a daughter somewhere in Long Beach by a Caucasian girl named Nichole. He went on to say she was super cute and looked just like me.

At first, I thought it was a joke. But then I remembered Nichole. I also remembered going to visit Nichole while I was with Michaelia and asking her if the child she had was mine. She had told me no then. As the years rolled by and this baby girl got older, Nichole must have realized I was the father.

I was excited about this. I wanted to know more instantly. I got her phone number and called her so we could set up a meeting. I told JuJu, Dirty Rat, Jay R and of course, my family. I also told a close female friend of mine named Maile. She offered to take me to meet this baby girl named Ariyonna. I would have asked Iris but we were almost done at this time so Maile was my best option.

I remember that day clearly. I was at Ab and JuJu's house in the valley. Maile was friends with the guys as well. She came to pick me up and drove me almost an hour away to Long Beach. I was very nervous but excitement took over. I wanted to be a father again.

When I pulled up to Nichole's mother's house, I saw her sitting on the porch. After Maile parked her car, we both got out and I introduced her to Nichole. Nichole asked if I wanted to see her. I said yes enthusiastically.

Let me tell you something, I had no idea you could love someone so quick and so fast. When Ariyonna walked out that front door and she looked at me eye to eye, the earth stopped spinning. I could feel baby Oscar smiling down on me from heaven. This girl, this angel, looked exactly like me except for the long hair and lighter skin. Nichole's mother, step-father, brothers and Maile all looked just as shocked and happy as I did. We all knew instantly that this was my child.

I immediately picked Ariyonna up (she was 3 years old at the time) and I told her I was her daddy. Nichole and I still did a paternity test just to be positive but we all knew this gorgeous specimen was a part of my DNA.

I started spending a lot of time with her. I was so proud to be a father again. I brought her to my parents' house often. I showed her off to all my friends. Everyone loved Ariyonna but not as much as I did.

After Iris and I broke up I really started hustling hard. I was doing a lot of illegal things but my most consistent trade was fraud. I was comfortable with it and really thought I was untouchable. I started making real money again so I decided to find a place.

I found out one of my singer friends named Billy (who was a close friend of Ne-Yo), was looking for a roommate. He had a condo in Winnetka off of Sherman Way and Cohasset Street. The area was slightly ghetto but the condo was nice. I moved in and started recording music with all my friends. I also started dating a lot of girls.

It's crazy to me now how close I was to success but I just couldn't focus without having sex. Even though I smoked a lot of marijuana and was starting to do cocaine more often, my worst addiction was sex. Through all of this God was still calling me but I kept ignoring His calls. I wanted everything my way or the fast way.

I had a Suburban Truck Limo with a driver and all. I should have had my own car but I didn't. What a waste of money. I didn't care. I was making 10-20 grand a week.

I was also still communicating with Jessica, but over time, we were almost completely done. I even flew to Milwaukee to visit her one more time but I had become another person. My ego was big and my talent was growing fast but I had no solid foundation.

I had too many friends in the industry but no complete circle. I was doing music with Lil Zane, Jay R, Shorty Mac, Detail, Fizz from B2K, Salim Grant, Brandon Howard, Jackie Jackson, Dirty Rat, Ab, JuJu and Sean Young. I had too much going on and no one to really slow me down because we were all either starts, or on the brink of stardom. I recorded some music with my roommate, Billy and I was starting to build a company with Dirty Rat and Lamont Bentley.

Then tragedy hit again. The night before this tragedy I spent some time with this very close friend. He was trying to patch some things up between me and Dirty Rat. We weren't speaking over something petty. After I saw him, I went out to hang with Sean Young. He took me to his actor friend Manye's house. Manye lived with his mother Pam who was a big casting agent. I had missed a few phone calls so one of my friends called Sean Young. It happened to be Shorty Mac, our mutual friend. That's when my world was interrupted once again when he said Lamont Bentley was dead.

I couldn't believe it. I had just seen Lamont the night before. But it was true. The same night I saw him he went home. Later that night he left to go run an errand and lost control of his car on the 118 freeway. He didn't have his seat belt on. He went through the sunroof and was run over by oncoming traffic.

This was a big blow for me. We were really building something strong and I trusted him. Death is a fact of life. I now have a better way of dealing with tragedy, not because I went through it, but because of my spiritual positions today.

You see, before I really gave my life to Christ, I took death and tragedy personally. When my son died, I blamed myself. When Sheila died, I blamed myself. When my grandmother died, I blamed myself but I also blamed God. I did all of this from a negative perspective. So when Lamont died, I took it personally and called myself cursed. Just when I felt my life making more sense and was motivated to succeed, I lost a real friend and ally in the entertainment business.

When I think about my life and this particular time, I realize that I didn't interact with my family very much. I still felt like an outcast. I also felt like I needed to make something of myself for them to love me again. I wonder how many people have allowed similar life choices to deter them from their dreams? How many get so trapped in their vices, they feel like they're too far gone? How many people turn their back on God when something goes wrong in their lives?

Let me tell you something that you may consider a cliched statement: *Life isn't fair, but God is good.* My father always said this in general and to my family when we were growing up. I never allowed this quote to mean much until I gave God His rightful place in my life as the head of it.

So, I hope you understand that at the death of Lamont a lot of me died at that time. I started doing a lot of cocaine and ecstasy.

After Iris, I jumped into a relationship with a girl named Chelsea who was young and willing to fulfill any sexual desire or fantasy I had. I took full advantage of this and used her to get closer to some of my industry friends by allowing her to be sexual with them.

I met Monique right after I moved in with Billy. I still hung onto Chelsea for a little longer, but Monique just had this very sensual way about her that trapped me instantly.

Monique and Chelsea were around 18 years old and barely legal. I was only a few years older, but that made me feel young again. I also met their mothers and continued building a bond with them.

I was meeting a large number of beautiful women who were very into me. Then one day when Cobra Red was braiding my hair, she reminded me this gift could make me money as well. I had already played with the escort lifestyle before, but this is when I took it to a larger level.

Cobra and I started collaborating with these women and making money off of them. I was also doing other fraudulent activity, which took my focus off of music.

I eventually severed my ties with Chelsea because I had stronger feelings for Monique. I had women escorting and doing check fraud so I was just too busy for more than one main girlfriend.

I still had the limo and the driver which started getting extremely expensive. I finally decided to buy a car and cut down the financial burden of a driver. Of course, it had to be a luxury car so I decided to get a BMW. I wanted a Lexus like the one I bought when baby Oscar died. But all that changed when I saw this silver M3 BMW.

Monique started doing a lot of things that broke our trust so I started spending less time with her. That's when Jennifer Lopez came into my life. Not to be confused with the superstar actress and singer. This Jennifer was a beautiful Italian woman from Northern California.

I was at the Archstone apartment complex visiting Jay R. I noticed her walking across the street as I was leaving. She was beautiful and carried herself with a strong element of class. I pulled up next to her and flirted with her. She responded with a smile and the rest is history.

Things got serious with Jennifer real fast. We were together every day. I introduced her to my closest friends at the time and everyone loved her. She was living at the Archstone, renting a room from a friend. As our relationship blossomed, she revealed more about herself to me. I realize now that she did it because of how open I was to her about how I made my money.

One day, we were at her place lying in bed and she revealed a few of her secrets to me. She told me she was on parole and she just got out of prison for fraud. I was instantly shocked and extremely turned on by what she told me. I felt like we were a perfect match so I asked her to marry me. She said yes and we planned a trip to Vegas to make it official.

Jennifer made me feel somewhat normal again. I felt like we would have a great marriage. She was understanding, seemed pretty honest, she was very beautiful and we got along really well. My daughter loved her and she treated Ariyonna like her own.

About a week before our wedding date, I got a call from a girl named Tasia who I used to date right before Iris. I had met her at Dirty Rat's video shoot and we slept together a few times. She eventually got pregnant and told me I was the father. I believed her because we had never used protection. We saw each other from time to time but then she lost her scholarship to Cal State Northridge and had to move back to San Diego. We didn't really have much in common and I didn't trust her at all.

OK, so back to the phone call. The purpose of this call was to tell me she was in labor. Thinking this was my child, I rushed to San Diego with Ariyonna to be there for her.

I made it down there in time for the baby's birth but something just didn't feel right. This kid looked nothing like me. He had freckles and was born with a 6th finger. I assumed Tasia had stronger genes and accepted him as mine. The decision would come back to haunt me for the next 11 years.

This was the summer of 2005 and I was about to become a married man. My music was coming out great and I was building some very strong relationships in the entertainment business as well. Jennifer was excited about becoming Mrs. Roberts and she did a lot to show me that she was my woman.

I decided to take a break from the escort business and focus on fraud, drug dealing and music.

It's very sad how this cute church going young man who used to pick roses from random gardens and bring them home to his mother is now living life like a mobster and gangster. I was so used to the man I became. I didn't think anything was wrong with me. Especially now that I was about to marry a woman who loved me just the way I was.

Right before we got on the road to Vegas, I let Jennifer use my car to run some errands. When she came back, she surprised me with both of our wedding bands and an envelope full of money. This made me fall in love with her even more. But was that love?

The drive to Vegas was smooth. We made it there in 3 hours. We rented a hotel room on the strip. We changed clothes and found a chapel to get married.

Before I continue with the wedding, I have to come back to the present for a brief venting session.

For the past couple of weeks, I've had a hard time getting my sister, Shamis, on the phone due to her busy schedule. All our lives we've been close, but when I found out the truth about my father, I pulled away from everyone. Even though everything happens for a reason I have had a hard time with guilt over neglecting her. The further I get away from my family, the more it affected my sister. She went through a very abusive relationship, started smoking cigarettes and she changed a lot. I don't need to get too deep about her personal life but this all ties into my story and faith tremendously.

With all the downfalls in my sister's life she is now a college graduate with two degrees from Long Beach State. She is a school teacher for kids with special needs, a photographer and she has a pretty secure position in the entertainment business.

Even though we've always been close, these past 19 months of my incarceration have brought us so much closer. We used to talk every other day. But lately, my funds have been low and she's been very busy. But last night we talked and I told her about this actor/model I wanted to manage named Garrett who is getting released tomorrow. Of course, she supported my decision and told me it was OK for him to call her about business. After we discussed this topic, she informed me that Cristal, the woman I'm still in love with texted her yesterday saying she wanted to come up here and surprise me with a visit.

You see, Cristal is one of the main reasons I'm writing my story. Right before I was arrested, I proposed to her. She said yes. I was arrested nine days later. For the first few months we talked a lot but then she turned really sour and broke my heart. Even though my relationship with Jesus Christ was developing nicely, Cristal leaving me broke me all the way down. I will go into more details later when I get to our season together but I just had to share these thoughts because they are happening right now.

Before I get back to Jennifer in Vegas let me tell you that being with Cristal made me realize I can love one woman and be totally satisfied with that. Of course, Cristal and I will never be together again but whoever God allows me to marry will definitely be blessed to have a real man of God who has been there and done that and who never wants to go back again.

Even though I'm living with no regrets, I can safely say if I were to do it all over again, I would stay a virgin until I got married. I would treat all women with supreme respect, especially my wife. For me, the only way to experience true love is by being true, real, and of course, honest and faithful to your significant other and your friends.

That's why I've changed my whole circle of friends and applied godly principles to my future approach to all relationships. I hope that through my story I can at least guide one person into this path of purity because it's the right way to be.

OK now back to 2005 and Vegas.

We found a wedding chapel and picked a package that came with our pictures on t-shirts, coffee mugs, etc. The wedding was quick. We said, "I do," and it was done. Jennifer was now my wife.

As I think about that day, she was very excited to be all mine, but I felt like something didn't add up. I didn't know why then, but I was soon to find out.

CHAPTER 5

When we got back to California, we started looking for a new place to live. I had told most of my close friends at that time about our marriage. I told Sean Young, Salim Grant, my boy KO, Lil Man, Zig, Dawn Monique, Jay R and a few others. I really started spending a lot of time with my daughter and really enjoyed being a father. I was also recording a lot of music and making money off my white collar activities. All of my focus was on everything but my relationship with God. I was still a believer but even the devil believes.

I believe that if I had died between 1998 and 2014, I would have gone straight to hell. This is only my opinion even though there are spiritual facts that have shown me I was hell bound. I was a terrible mix of good hearted and evil minded. That way of living and thinking reflected the type of friends I associated with and the women I tried to love. I was so used to drastic change at this time of my life that this next turn of events only made me colder hearted.

I still had a parole officer at this time. So did my new wife. I was on great terms with my parole office. My wife was in pretty good rapport with her PO, too.

One morning, while I was hanging out with my daughter and Sean, my wife received a call from her parole officer. She was told to check in immediately. I don't fully recall my reason for not being able to go but I think I had to pick-up some money. Sean didn't have any sessions scheduled that day with his girlfriend, singer Tiffany Villareal. He offered to watch my daughter and give my wife a ride to her PO. I gave my wife and daughter a kiss good-bye and went to handle business.

I received a call from Sean 30 minutes later telling me my wife was arrested by her PO. I was extremely shocked because I didn't think my wife was involved in any criminal acts. Obviously, I was very wrong.

Jennifer was charged with fraud. But that's not the worst part. My wife was still married to this wealthy guy from Napa Valley and they had a young child together. She was so into me that she used one of his corporate checking accounts from a restaurant he owned. She took thousands of dollars from it and gave it to me.

Due to my criminal lifestyle this didn't bother me as much as the fact she was already married. That made our marriage invalid.

I thought I had finally found someone to love, but nope. It was all a figment of my imagination. Now she was going back to prison and I was back to being the dog/player I was accustomed to being anyway.

Right before Jennifer's arrest, we found an apartment in North Hollywood. The area wasn't that great but the price was lovely and we didn't have to fill out any applications. The owner loved us, especially my daughter. My daughter has always been beautiful, but in her younger years, she would make people do amazing things for us just by asking. People found it very hard to say no to her. We went to Ikea to shop for the apartment and had the place furnished in two days.

My daughter's fourth birthday was coming up in the next few months so I started planning early. This would be my first birthday with her so I had to make sure it was epic. In between planning her birthday and making money, I was recording and networking with a lot of people.

Dawn Monique had connected me with Mike Williams, a producer/ engineer. He had a lovely studio in Malibu up the hill from the biker/ seafood restaurant, Neptunes Net. Mike's studio was and still is called The Krunchy Barn. He gave me all access and we started recording a lot of music together.

My boy Salim Grant connected me with Jackie Jackson and he allowed me to work in his studio as well. At that time his label was called Jesco Records and he had David Esterson as his head of A&R. Jackie also had my good friend Brandon Howard as one of his producers and my boy Deja from Subliminal Records had a studio connected to his. Jay R was also a big part of this circle of friends but he spent most of his time at Edmonds Towers recording with his group and the production squad, The Underdogs.

So I was connected with Tank, Jon B, Steve from the group Troop, Luke James and his brother Q, Bernard Alexander, Mark Sparkx, Kevin Backstrom, Tracy Edmonds and many more through Jay R. He was signed to Yab Yum and J Records at the time.

Only God knows why I didn't explode to the next level then. But I know what mainly held me back- myself.

I was all over the place. I had too many friends who didn't really appreciate what I brought to the table. I was so excited most of the time and I was making my own money so I didn't force much business to benefit my career. All of these people knew I was talented. I actually had real records that they loved. But everyone was too busy doing their own thing to focus on me. Jay R and Salim truly believed in me and we made so many amazing records together. I could put one of them out now in 2017 and people would think we just recorded it. 2005 was a great year for me musically but my heart was so damaged and it just kept getting worse and worse.

About two months before Ariyonna's 4th birthday, Salim invited me to a session at Jackie's studio. He had this singer named Tiffany Sayers coming as well. He had told me about her before and showed me pictures. She was extremely beautiful, about 5'4", blue eyes, very physically fit and pretty little feet like a princess. I've always had a fetish for pretty feet, especially French tips. Ooh-wee!

I was super excited about getting to meet her, especially after my short-lived marriage to Jennifer. I had started sleeping with Monique again and this rich girl named Melissa Macintosh but for some reason, Tiffany had my full attention.

At that time, she drove a blue Honda Civic. I remember her pulling into the studio parking lot. Salim and I were in my Beamer smoking marijuana and doing a few lines of cocaine. When this woman got out of that car in that low cut shirt and those tight blue jeans, with those open toed shoes and French tipped nail and toes- I was done. This woman was so gorgeous and her attitude was so sweet and carefree. I told Salim that day that she was going to be my girl very soon.

We went into the studio and had fun vibing together. I played Tiffany some of my music and she loved it a lot. We exchanged numbers and hung out a few more times at a couple of different studio sessions. One evening, at one of the sessions, I made a very strong move on her and she didn't push me away. We didn't go past intense kissing but it was obvious we had a very powerful connection. Even though I wanted to be in a relationship with Tiffany, she played hard to get. Due to her making me work for a more intimate encounter, I kept my sexual desires met by Monique and Melissa but my heart was never with any of these women.

One day I had a get together at my house. I had Monique there and I invited Tiffany as well. All of my guy friends were interested in them both but I didn't really think that much about anyone but Tiffany.

After people started leaving, I was relaxing in my bed next to Monique. Tiffany just came and got on top of me and started kissing me intently. Monique got really mad and left and the rest was history. From then on, Tiffany was all mine.

I feel guilty as I think about it now how I used Monique to make Tiffany jealous but I must say it worked perfectly. From that day in late April 2005 Tiffany Sayers was my new woman.

The bible says you reap what you sow. Let me tell you something from my heart. Not all of my adversities were deserved but many of them were because of my bad intentions and selfish ways.

Did I love Tiffany? Yes. Or so I thought at the time. As I reflect on my life in my present state of mind, I realize I didn't love myself and most importantly, I didn't love God. I tried to use God and manipulate Him to fit into my lifestyle.

Some of you who read this story may have many questions about some of the people and experiences I didn't elaborate on more. I want you to understand that this is my testimony. It's more than a life story. This is also about my struggles finding love and developing real friendships and relationships. Most importantly, my story is being shared to give God the glory and hopefully help people who have walked down some of the same or similar paths and let them know they are not too far gone to be forgiven and redeemed. If any of you have ever read the Biblical story about the prodigal son, this is just a very long version of it.

OK, now back to Tiffany.

Like many of the women in my life, Tiffany was a great woman. She had recently graduated from Long Beach State. She was very beautiful. She was talented and she believed in me. She also believed in God, which made me very comfortable sharing my faith with her. As soon as we became a couple, we started writing songs together and recording as well. My daughter loved her instantly and they shared a beautiful connection. Shortly after Tiffany and I got together my daughter's 4th birthday approached.

I went all out for this special day because it would be my first birthday with Ariyonna. We had the party at Balboa Park. I ordered the super jumper with double slides, a caterer, and a stretch limo. I invited some of my closest friends at the time and we all had a ball. Ariyonna really enjoyed herself and she made me really proud to be her father. She filled the void from losing baby Oscar and reduced a lot of the guilt and pain I was holding onto. After the birthday party, we all said our good-byes. Tiffany, Ariyonna and I took the limo back to my home.

Tiffany and I got really close, real fast. I reduced my illegal activities and stopped seeing other women as well. I still did drugs at the time and I slowly started losing everything. My personality seemed to split but the music continued to grow. Most of my industry friends loved Tiffany so I continued to allow her to record music in a lot of my sessions.

After a few months of being together, I got evicted from my apartment. I still had my BMW so I wasn't completely broke. Tiffany allowed me to move into her apartment in Long Beach with her and her roommate.

Tiffany worked at a restaurant called BJ's. Even though she had her degree and a career path she wanted to be a singer. Her roommate was also a musician so Tiffany's drive wasn't distracted by anyone on a different path. This is what she wanted to do.

A social media music site called MySpace was really popular at the time. Since I had so much music, it was easy for me to set up my page and upload music to it. But for Tiffany, we still had more work to do so we started recording more songs geared toward her musical genre. Even though I didn't have a set income, I always had studio time somewhere. Then things started getting more serious for me as an artist.

I started working with a producer named Anthony Ransome from Baltimore. He and his wife had recently moved to Los Angeles. His wife was a computer genius and a very professional business woman with wonderful business etiquette. We instantly became close. Anthony was tied to Motown/Universal and he had a few projects he was working on. He actually paid me for a couple of verses on this Gorrilaz tribute album and he involved me on this military compilation called Voices From the Front Line.

From the beginning of our friendship, we expressed our faith in God and each other. This foundation is something I should have paid closer attention to back then because as I sit in prison writing this, besides my family, Anthony and his wife Pilar are the only friends I have in my corner when I needed them the most. We are going on 12 years strong and all I can say is, glory to God.

Friendships and relationships are very important in life. Without them we can easily fall into the wrong lifestyles with the wrong types of friends. That can happen as well.

Ok, now back to Tiffany.

We made it to 2006 and we were a very close couple. We were recording a lot in Malibu as a couple/team and I was doing a lot with Anthony and Salim as well. I was still hustling but nothing like before and I was still doing good with my parole officer Mr. Barnes. The music was growing but Tiffany and I started to grow apart.

A few elements to this equation was me living with her and our drug habits. As much as I loved Tiffany it was becoming a problem between us as artists because I was so hard on her.

One day when she was at work, I was on MySpace checking my messages and I noticed one from a very familiar face. After about five years and breaking my heart Valerie Mamane had found me on MySpace. She reached out to me and told me to call her.

As crazy as this sounds to me now, I wasn't over Valerie and as soon as I heard her voice a ton of emotions were ignited all over again. Valerie was a woman now and attending Cal State Northridge. She was working at a BBQ restaurant called Woodranch. Everything with Valerie started as a slow process because I still didn't trust her fully. I also had a piece of resentment towards her for leaving me the way that she did. We talked often and I told her about the death of my son who was alive when we were together.

One day, Tiffany and I had a session with Mike Williams in Malibu and Krunchy Barn Recording Studios. I made plans with Valerie to meet up on PCH at Starbucks not too far from the studio. I also told Valerie I was single and wanted us to be together again. Of course, this was a lie because Tiffany was still my girlfriend at the time. Once the studio session got going and Tiffany got in the booth, I made up a reason to go run an errand. I drove so fast because I figured Valerie was already waiting on me and I was right.

When I pulled up, she was sitting in her white Nissan Maxima drinking a Chai Latte, her favorite drink, with soy milk, of course. When I pulled up next to her, we locked eyes and my heart sank somewhere into the abyss. Valerie was so much more beautiful than I remembered and I was in trouble for sure.

We talked that night for an hour or two and caught up on so much more. I showed her pictures of Ariyonna. She showed me her nephews. We kissed and I felt a big surge of guilt run through my veins. I knew then that I was going to have to find a way to leave Tiffany without breaking her heart.

In my twisted mind I thought this was fate bringing Valerie back to me. Obviously, I was wrong because I'm sitting here in prison with no woman to call my own and a whole bunch of emotional scars due to my lack of obedience to what God wanted me to do with my life.

We are still in 2006 but this year would end with a super bang and not a good one.

Halloween was fun. Ariyonna dressed up as a princess and I took her to a few nice children's events. Tiffany and I were still together and Valerie and I were much closer to being a couple as well. Ariyonna had so much fun and then I took her home to her mom so they could go trick-or-treating. That night Tiffany and I went to a party and really enjoyed ourselves. The next day I had plans to see Valerie again.

The next morning went like normal. I walked Tiffany to her car as she was on her way to work. I had plans to stay with Valerie that night and I was very excited because we had just started being intimate again.

I know people get away with lying and cheating often and so did I.

But it's wrong to be so selfish and intentionally hurt others.

So, I got in my car and got on the 405 south to the 605 headed towards my mother's house to pick something up before going to Sherman Oaks, where Valerie lived. I wasn't driving fast, but I was driving in the carpool lane, which is illegal if you have no passengers, which I didn't. After driving on the 605 for about 5 or 10 minutes my life changed very quickly once again.

As I was driving in the carpool lane a car driving in the fast lane lost control and hit me as we were going 70 mph. I instantly lost control and hit the center divider which made my car flip 5 or 6 times. I was also hit by a couple of other cars and a big diesel truck. I think it was an 18-wheeler. Of course, I had my seat belt on, but honestly, that's not what saved me. God saved me because he had a purpose for my life.

I climbed out the window of my BMW without a scratch. The car was crushed like a soda can. Everyone on the freeway, including the ambulance and the police were so surprised to see me standing without a problem. I was only one exit away from my mother's house. Also, some people at the Cerritos Mall who saw my car flipping ran to help me, expecting me to be injured but I wasn't at all.

The paramedics still took me to the hospital to run some tests on me and make sure I didn't have internal problems. My daughter's mother Nichole came to see me immediately with Ariyonna and so did Tiffany. Valerie would have come as well but I didn't call her until a little later.

Let me tell you how much grace God gives to human beings in hopes that we choose to believe in Him and do good in life. I didn't fully appreciate the blessing until now. I took God for granted and expected him to do everything I wanted him to do for me. I also took for granted my amazing family and church who have been praying for me in so many ways. Even though God called me to be an evangelist, I had to answer the call and live accordingly. Even though I'm in prison, I'm practicing this way of living. I'm being obedient to God's Word and rebuilding my heart to love everyone, even if I don't like them.

You would think that from having a near death experience I would at least change a little bit, but honestly, I got worse. Shortly after this accident, Tiffany and I decided to be friends with benefits and I moved out of her apartment. Valerie and I started being more serious and I started hustling a lot more because I didn't have a car anymore. I kept recording more and searching for more opportunities to further my music career.

That's when I met Gary, a Filipino businessman investing in this young artist, Sean Kingston. I first met Gary and Sean at a clothing store on Lankershim Blvd in North Hollywood owned by Max, a close friend of mine. Max was a powerful Jamaican who shared a lot of the same friends that I had at the time. Max told me to show Sean Kingston around LA and he also told Gary that he should get to know me.

Sean and I instantly got along and we hung out often at the time. Gary also liked being around me and we started spending a lot of time together as well. Gary was a big Tupac fan so anything dealing with rap music caught his attention. After about two weeks of building with Gary, he offered to get me an apartment in Studio City at the Archstone where Jay R, Ricky Romance, Bijon and P Gordy were staying. Even though I knew many other people who lived in this complex, these few guys were with me a lot after I moved in.

Because I now lived in the valley, Valerie and I started getting closer and closer. Tiffany and I were still being intimate as well, especially because she had recently moved to Hollywood, right off the 101 and Gower Street. She was really serious about her music by now and she got a job as a bottle service girl at a nightclub.

I still didn't have a car so Gary got me a black C-Class Mercedes Benz. I think it was a 320 series. Gary also bought me a Canon video camera from Fry's Electronics and gave me a few thousand dollars. Once again, I slowed down my illegal activities and really focused on my music.

That's when I started working with CJ Hilton from Baltimore. CJ was a singer/producer who was young and extremely talented. He was signed to Capital Records and had a pretty big record deal. I also got asked to be in a rap group called Outlandizh by my good friend P Gordy. P. Gordy and Desmond "Big Dez" Mapp had started this group together. P. Gordy was the manager and Big Dez was one of the artists and also the producer of the project. Big Dez was already an established producer. He produced many multi-platinum hits with Master P and other artists as well.

This all occurred in the fall of 2006. Just that fast I went from no home and no car to a luxury apartment, a luxury car and a large amount of celebrity contacts in my immediate circle.

My ego was so twisted at this time and I just felt untouchable. I didn't respect women at all and I took the ones in my life for granted. Even though a lot of artists in the same position I was in succeeded, God obviously had a very different plan for my future.

After living at the Archstone for a couple of months, my relationship with Gary started to crumble because he was battling very serious mental issues and his wife started shutting down everything that he and I had built together.

First to go was the Mercedes, which she got back from me by threatening me with the police who actually called my phone. Me being on parole and close to actually completing my parole sentence at that time, I reacted pretty quickly when the detective called me. He told me that Gary's wife reported the car stolen and Gary was actually admitted to a mental hospital. He instructed me to drop the car off at a public location and to leave the keys in the car.

At first, my reaction was to dismiss all of this and keep the car, but thank God my logical mindset was intact and I complied with the detectives' request. I kept the apartment until I was evicted which was around October. P Gordy lived in the same complex on the very expensive side that had lofts. He offered to rent me the loft space and I immediately moved in.

By this time, the new rap group I was in was recording a lot of songs. We had recently recorded a record with Too-Short. One of the rappers, Big Dez, had a strong relationship with him because he produced multiple records on his albums. My sound was a great addition to the group and I also brought a lot of connections to the table so P Gordy had no problem making me his roommate.

By now, Valerie was officially my girlfriend again and I was seeing Tiffany about once a week or every other week. One of my other friends at that time, a rapper named Lil Zane started dating my ex Monique. She brought her and one of her friends around, this girl named Yanira. As occupied as I was with women, I was slightly jealous of Zane and Monique but I didn't let it show. Me being such a sexual deviant,

I flirted with her friend, Yanira and we started having a sexual relationship.

Not that I regret sleeping with her in general but I wish I didn't sleep with anyone until I became a godly, married man. It's not worth it to spread yourself so thin at any given moment to sexual desires.

My group Outlandizh started doing shows and Big Dez and I started collaborating on a lot of projects. I started bringing my friends to collab with Dez often. I brought Sean Young, Sean Kingston, Bijon, CJ Hilton and comedian/actor Miguel Nunez to the studio. Everyone got along great and Dez and I started to create a strong bond. At that time, I was so focused on being an artist, I didn't realize my networking abilities could have easily created a lot of revenue for me then. But I was stuck on friendship and the old school handshake way of doing business. I didn't have contracts with anyone to properly protect my interests.

It's amazing when I think back to this time and I see how successful most of these people are today. Even though they know who I am, they have never shared any of the fruits of their success even though I helped many of them in many ways, especially financially. Even though I made my money the wrong way, I still made it and I gave a lot to my friends in many different situations.

The lesson for all of you hustlers out there is first, hustle legally.

Second, choose your friends wisely. Fast money goes just as fast as it comes.

OK, now my life started taking different turns.

P Gordy was getting evicted from his place but we were still doing business together. Him and Dez decided to get a really nice place in Sherman Oaks around the corner from Valerie's house. Even though I knew I could stay with them, I was not too interested in living with anyone else at that time so I decided to move in with Valerie.

I had recently got a Nissan Pathfinder so I was able to get around. And I was still making a little money doing what I did on the side. I spent a lot of time in Hollywood and Beverly Hills because I knew that was where the people, I liked to associate with spent their time as well. That's when I met Stella, this Russian beauty queen who worked at I.H.O.P. on Santa Monica Blvd.

After the first time I met her, I made it a habit of going there when she worked just to see her smile. She actually had a boyfriend at the time but I was still able to get her phone number by using my piquancy. For those who aren't familiar with the word, that means my magnetic charm.

Even though I was with Valerie, I was also being pretty promiscuous. Stella made me feel something inside that I've never actually felt with any woman before or after her. What's even stranger is that Stella and I never had a sexual relationship. We kissed twice and we've been on a couple dates. She's met my family and my daughter and they all love her.

Not to go off subject, but Stella believes in God. She's a very loyal friend and she's extremely honest. Even though Stella and I were never boyfriend and girlfriend, we've stayed in contact with each other for almost 11 years.

At the prison I'm currently serving time in, we aren't in two-man cells like the one I was at in Victorville. This prison is a low security facility. I'm in a dorm with about 140 bunk beds. Even though my bunkmate is white and in here for child pornography, we have a very brotherly bond and I've allowed him to read this story so far. The reason I'm sharing this with you readers is because of the important lessons that may jump right out to some of you, but for you all that don't get it, pay attention.

After my bunkmate Steve read my story so far, he made a couple of strong comments and suggestions. First, he said that whatever woman I end up marrying after she reads this story has to be a very special woman with thick skin and high godly morals. Second, he said that my story made him think about his life and he shared some of his memories with me. He also suggested that I continue, and stay the course.

That's why Stella's friendship with me and him being in my life must be told. Even though I loved Cristal, who was the woman I proposed to before I came to jail, who has left me and went out of her way to hurt me. She totally ignored over 100 letters I've written to her being positive, godly and honest. She blames me for everything and has lied to me for no reason. Yet I still love her. Not the love for a wife, but the agape love of God which is unconditional.

You see, not to get off track with the pace and time of my life story, I must share this now even though we will cross the bridge a little deeper as we get to the 2013- 2014 era of my life. But for now, let me explain this cross between Stella and Cristal.

When I met Stella, I had one child, my daughter Ariyonna. Now I have 5 children by 5 different women. None of these women were ever my girlfriend. It was all sexual.

When I proposed to Cristal in December of 2014, I went to jail nine days later. A couple of months before that, Cristal had a horrible miscarriage and our child was lost. Before the miscarriage, we had broken up and I spent a whole day with Stella.

For the past 11 years, one of us is single when the other one is in a serious relationship. When we spent that day together, we talked about my relationship with Cristal and we talked about us actually being together. Stella has always made me realize that being with her would not happen overnight like I'm used to with almost all of my other relationships. No human being is perfect but there is someone for everyone. I've learned this the hard way.

When I actually proposed to Cristal, in the back of my mind, I was wishing it was Stella. I've held onto my feelings for Stella for a long time. I even wrote her a 5-page letter that I sent to my mother to hold for me because I didn't have Stella's address. Not many women are built to stay with a man while he's in prison so I don't blame Cristal for it. I'm actually thankful.

I'm closer to God than I've ever been. I have a better appreciation for all women, especially the of women I've encountered in the past 20 years. I've allowed God to take control and I'm not going to rush anything at all. But you can be 100% certain that I will cherish and adore and most importantly respect the future Mrs. Roberts. I will love her the way God intended every man to love his woman.

Like the Bible says in Genesis 2:That is why a man leaves his father and mother and is united to his wife, and they become one flesh.

Also, the apostle Paul quotes this same verse in Ephesians 5:31-33 but he goes deeper, comparing this unit to Jesus Christ and the church.

church. **33** However, each one of you also must love his wife as he loves himself, and the wife must respect her husband.

This is another reason why I'm sharing my life story and the battles I've had with love, fidelity, drugs, money, abuse and simply put, pain.

So back to late fall, almost winter of 2006.

Stella was in my life, but she was in a committed relationship. I was living with Valerie and still sleeping with Tiffany and Monique's friend Yanira. There were others as well, but there's no need to explain every encounter. But basically, I was a dog, player, liar, cheater and manipulator. Not to justify anything but I was extremely damaged goods with multiple personalities and a serious ego.

As 2007 approached, Valerie and I got very, very serious. We also started having real couple issues. Even though she pushed me to pursue my dreams, she wanted me to keep her on a pedestal. Valerie was too good for me at that time, but for some reason, we were still together.

In March of 2007, Big Dez decided he wanted our group to move to Houston, Texas to build our fan base since we had a southern sound and he was originally from Galveston, Texas. We had a 3rd group member named Tay. He didn't want to move. Neither did P Gordy although P Gordy thought it would be a good idea to make the transition.

At this time, Valerie and I still weren't on the same page and the girl I had slept with a few times, Yanira, was pregnant. Due to Yanira's lifestyle, I didn't think I was the father. So, I totally shut her out of my life and focused on myself. This would actually turn out to be my first son since the death of baby Oscar and a beautiful baby boy named Joell.

I decided to go with Big Dez to Houston and build on our group Outlandizh and network our way into something great. The hardest part for me and Dez was leaving our daughters because they were so close to us. Valerie supported me and we planned to make our relationship work long distance.

CHAPTER 6

Dez and I packed our belongings late spring of 2006 and drove his black Chevy truck to Texas. We didn't have much money so we decided to drive straight there. Dez had a contract with a small, independent record company in Houston. Due to the relationship between this company and I, their name isn't coming back to me. But the beginning of the business relationship started off OK.

They put us up in a Motel 6 and gave us access to their recording studio. Dez had multiple platinum and gold plaques. We decorated the studio walls with them. The record label had a few artists they wanted us to develop. Due to Dez's southern reputation with hit records like, I Got the Hook Up, I Miss My Homies, Ghetto D, and his group, the Sons of Funk, their artists were eager to work with us.

Dez and I were a very good team. I knew how to network and write lyrics. He knew how to produce hit records and write lyrics as well. I was a very outgoing person. Dez was very laid back. Together, we took Houston by storm.

Of course, I started meeting a lot of women and Dez loved that about me. Valerie and I talked on the phone every day but I had an out of sight, out of mind type attitude. Eventually Dez and I got a nice two-bedroom apartment on the outskirts of Houston next to Pearland in a gated community. It took me no time to make friends and connect with promoters and other artists. Our group Outlandizh really started to blossom as the months passed by.

My Ariyonna's birthday came in June. Valerie offered to buy me a plane ticket so I could spend her 5th birthday with her. Of course, I accepted her nice gesture and went to be with them. I spent a week in California and had a ball with Ariyonna and Valerie. But little did I know Valerie and I would not be a couple anymore after that trip.

When I got back to Houston, I really changed for the worse in many ways. At that time, none of my current reflections of myself existed. To me, I was on top of the world. I was working closely with a multi-platinum producer. We were taking over a new city. I had my choice of women and I was building a name for myself as an artist.

Southern hospitality is actually a true definition of the south because people weren't used to California based entertainers relocating. I really lost myself in this environment. I had more than one girl I was seeing regularly but none of them were serious to me.

Valerie decided to totally end our relationship because she found out I was sleeping with girls and recording it on my camera phone. Somehow, she hacked into my Verizon account and my email and actually watched me be intimate with another woman unprotected. I tried to lie my way out of it, but I was caught red-handed. That was the end of us.

As I think about it now, my relationship with Valerie was rooted in revenge and resentment from her leaving me broken hearted. So, when she called me crying and upset, I wasn't even affected by her emotions. I felt she got what she deserved, which was very wrong on my part because two wrongs don't make a right. I should have stayed with Tiffany and built a solid lasting relationship instead of moving too fast for what I thought was love, but was really lust. Now I was free to be a dog and I did that very well.

I started getting women to do everything for me and Dez and I mean *everything*. We shared women sexually, they cooked, cleaned and they paid our rent. They drove me anywhere I wanted to go. They flew in from other states or drove to be with us. They were objects of necessity instead of being what God intended for them to be.

Late into the fall of 2007 we decided to add a few members to our group. We brought in Kano, a pretty successful Texas rapper, and a young Nola, from New Orleans. My boy JuJu connected us with some investors from San Antonio. We had already recorded most of the records before adding these members. All they had to do was write versus and fill in a place on the track.

There was a big director named Mr. Boomtown who shot a lot of the big videos for artists like Bun B and Slim Thug. I decided to reach out to him to direct the video for our single called, *Touch Me.*

I had been working with this girl named Nicole on computer graphics and logos for the CD and we became intimate. This sexual endeavor would be the creation of my

2nd son Taven. Of course, I wasn't thinking about children while I was being sexual with my children's mothers, but God doesn't make any mistakes.

Me, Dez, and the main investor, Slim, decided it would be best to rent a house in Pearland where Bun B lived because our apartment was too small for such a big group. We looked for a few days until we found a nice, big, four-bedroom house. Dez and I put the place in our name. We started promoting our single with the Go DJ's. We also set a date to shoot the video with Mr. Boomtown.

Since I introduced Sean Young to Dez they had started to become close so Sean decided to come to Houston and network with us. I was so blinded by friendship and other distractions I never put it together until now how much Sean used me to get close to my connections but never really bothered to connect me with some of his. He wasn't the only one who took advantage of my networking qualities and profited from them. Many of my friends my family didn't approve of because they could see all the things I couldn't. But regardless, I've learned so much through my ups and downs. I am a lot stronger and wiser because of it.

OK, now back to Houston.

We shot the video in the sprint of 2007. By that time, our song was getting played in all the clubs in Houston and on the radio. We were doing all of this without any major or independent record label. All we had was an investor and our radio promotion personnel. We were missing a lot of important components to really make this takes off. That's when we realized we should move to Atlanta to create a bigger buzz and network with the record labels out there. We decided to pack our things, drive to California to see our daughters, then drive to Atlanta to continue to create a legacy. Sean Young decided to move with us as well. Seemed like a great idea at the time. So we drove to Los Angeles and spent about a week with our children and spent time with family and friends.

The time had passed by so quickly and now we were in the beginning of 2008. I was now the father of three children. Yanira and Joell were living in California at the time and Tavern and Nicole were still in Houston. Ariyonna and her mother Nichole were still living in Long Beach as well. I wasn't communicating with Tavern's mom at the time. So I didn't even know I had a new son yet. Yanira had tracked me down through some of my friends. I think I got a chance to see Joell once at this time.

The move to Atlanta went smooth and we found a nice, three-bedroom apartment in Sandy Springs right outside of Atlanta. Sean and I made the transition pretty easily but Dez didn't like it that much. Eventually, Dez decided to move back to Los Angeles while Sean and I stayed.

Atlanta was perfect for what we were doing musically and the women loved us. I also started doing a lot of my old white collar activities so I maintained a steady income.

I got involved in two serious relationships while I was in Atlanta. One was with an industry executive named Katrina Young. The other was with property manager Kateri Gorney.

Katrina and I met before Dez moved back to Los Angeles and we became a couple pretty quickly. We also became engaged after about two months of dating. We were destined for failure once I got to know her and realized how evil and toxic she became after a bottle of wine. I tried to make it work with her, but not for the right reasons.

You see, this woman knew a lot of powerful people and she was very close to Blue Williams, who managed Nick Cannon, Big Sean and other celebrities. Also, we had a strong sexual chemistry and we got along great-when she was sober. Sean wanted me to make it work but even he knew it wouldn't last. Right before the summer of 2008, we were done.

Not even a week later, I met Kateri at one of Atlanta's biggest nightclubs. I was in VIP and we locked eyes as she was on her way out of the club. I was able to catch her before she left and we instantly hit it off. That same night I was at her place and the rest is history.

Kateri was a southern bell for real and a big difference from Katrina. Kateri had two beautiful boys named King and Tecori. My feelings for her developed really fast. We were like a family. I became very close with her mother and we all spent a lot of time together.

In between these two romantic relationships with these women, I also met two very talented individuals I am still associated with today. One is a very talented producer, Chuck "Chalo" Hester. The other is artist/songwriter Derek "Dsmoove" Fredie. Chalo was from Chicago and Dsmoove was from New York. I met Chalo through Katrina because she was trying to help me find more producers to work with on my solo project. At that time, Chalo had just produced a pretty big single called "Amilli," by Lil Wayne.

Chalo and I instantly got along and started recording music together. He was happily married and a very devoted husband. Our connection was similar to the one I still have with Anthony and his wife Pilar. Very spiritual and honest.

Now my friendship with Dsmoove was totally different. I met him in Sandy Springs. He was my neighbor and we started off as smoking buddies. Then one day he told me about his singing group, Red Dirt. They were signed to Upfront Management, one of Akon's companies. He was also related to Sean "Puffy" Combs and had many other industry ties. Dsmoove and I were both ladies' men and we had a similar love for money. So, we started building in multiple areas.

By this time, Dez was in the process of moving back to Los Angeles. He and Dsmoove got a chance to meet and collaborated on some music. For some reason Dsmoove and Sean Young didn't connect that well. I think their personalities just clashed so they never really built a friendship.

I was so caught up in my new relationship with Kateri I barely had time for anyone. I really thought Kateri and I were going to be together for a long time. I changed quickly and stopped seeing other girls. But I also became very insecure and possessive of her, which was very odd for me.

The beginning was magical. Kateri let down her walls and trusted me with her children and her home. I had my own place but I spent a lot of time at hers.

In 2008 we decided to take a trip to southern California to visit my family and so I could show her around Los Angeles. My family loved her and her children and the trip was mostly fun. The only downside was my finances. I was expecting some money situations to go through that never happened, which meant Kateri would have to pay for most of the trip. She definitely didn't like that at all.

When we got back to Atlanta, we started having problems mainly because I wasn't making much money. That's when I started getting more possessive and Kateri started getting sneaky and very secretive. In the beginning of our relationship, we were intimate pretty often, but now it was very hard to get her to be as affectionate as she used to be. As embarrassing as this is, I must be truthful because I know men and women do this.

One night, before our relationship was over, she invited me to bed. I was excited but still sad because she wanted me to use a condom. Instead of being consistent with her wishes, I ripped a hole in the condom because I wanted to get her pregnant. For some reason, she could tell something wasn't right. She stopped me, checked the condom and found the hole. She got mad and asked me to leave. We never recovered from that.

Honesty is important in all relationships as well as trust. And just because we barely used protection in the beginning of our relationship didn't give me the right to make a decision for both of us. It's so sad I fell so low in an attempt to keep this girl. Of course, I apologized. She eventually forgave me but we were never intimate again and we never went back to being a couple.

You would think I would have learned from this and slowed down- but no- I became even worse. My heart was so twisted. I started dating many women and hustling intensely again. I had to do something to get my mind off Kateri because I was still extremely into her.

At that time, I was still working with Chalo. The record he did with Lil Wayne was a big hit. I introduced him to Sean Young, who was close to Livio Harris, an executive at a publishing company in Hollywood. Even though I knew Livio very well, especially because he was the manager of my longtime neighbor and friend Jonathon "Lil J" McDaniel, I trusted Sean to do the right thing when the deal went through for Chalo's publishing on this record. But I was wrong.

Sean, being greedy, received $5,500 for his percentage. He gave me $500 bucks. That's actually the first and only time he's given me a percentage for something I connected him to. After this, my eyes were opened to what he and others really thought about my worth so I started preparing for a big change once again.

After Sean did this I came into some very nice money and I gave him $5,000 even after what he did to me. Sean, being greedy, didn't fully appreciate it when he found out I made $40,000 but I didn't care. I had to take care of myself first.

Of course, two wrongs don't make a right and I was just as wrong as he was but at that time, I felt justified. Plus, I had other people to take care of and I was planning to move back to LA to work with DC2 and Lil J on music.

Dez and P Gordy actually had these awards show performance booked and DC2 invited me to perform on the song. My younger brother Tamrin, aka Universal, was really getting good at rapping so I asked him to write my verse for the song. Dez and P Gordy loved the verse so we were set to do this event. I was so excited to perform again. I bought tickets for my whole family to come.

At this time, Stella was a server at a high-end restaurant on Sunset in West Hollywood. I took my family out to eat there and that was the first time they met her. All of the feelings I used to have for her came back instantly so I invited her to be my date to the show. I also offered to buy her a dress and shoes and to get her pampered really nice for the show. She said yes and I was a very happy man.

Everything went as planned. We shopped at the Beverly Center. I got a nice hotel room on Sunset close to the event and I couldn't wait to show Stella off to my family and friends.

The event was held on Hollywood and Highland at the Level 4 location. My whole family showed up. My father brought his camera and took lots of pictures. I reserved a table for us all to sit together. Stella instantly got along with everyone and I finally felt like I was going to make her my girlfriend. My performance with Dez was amazing and we received a great response from everyone. I also networked a little and spent the rest of the time with Stella and my family.

One of my friends I met in Atlanta, Daryl Easterling aka Tiger da Writer, a singer/songwriter kept coming to mind because I was meeting a lot of singers and he and I worked well together. I remember thinking about building some type of A&R management company with him.

As much as my mind was on business, it was also on Stella and the rest of our evening together. After the event was over, I said good-bye to my family. I got in the car with Stella to go back to my hotel on Sunset Blvd. I was really looking forward to finally spending the night with her, but that never happened. Instead, when we pulled up to my hotel Stella told me good-night and said she had to go home. I instantly got upset. I tried to convince her to stay but she said she had to work early and that she had a great time with me tonight. So once again, Stella rejected me and I was super crushed. I was so used to girls mostly doing what I wanted. I just couldn't grasp the fact that Stella was different.

I only had a few days left before flying back to Atlanta. I met up with Monte, a close friend in real estate about moving back to LA. He was currently living in Encino in a very luxurious house that had a nice bedroom with a bathroom and balcony included and was available for me to rent. I told him to reserve this place for me and gave him a deposit.

Next, I went to see Teddy Riley about some music opportunities and spent some time with my boy Lil J. I still wasn't 100% sure about completely leaving Atlanta because I really got along with a lot of people out there. But California was my home and I was home sick.

My last night I went out with Lil Man from my hood in Inglewood, KD and Don Dada, my boy from the Bay who was big on the Hollywood promo scene. We always had a lot of fun when we were all together and we also did a lot of extra-curricular activities. These were my boys and had been for years.

My flight back to Atlanta was smooth. Sean Young and I were still roommates but our friendship was changing quickly. I just started seeing him for what he really was and I was over it. He wasn't the only friend who took me for granted but he was the one who did it the most.

As I sit here and think about the 21 years, I've known him it was definitely one helluva ride. I've learned so much with him as well as from him. We had great times, we had sad times, we had rough times, and of course, we are where we are now. He knows I'm in prison and he hasn't reached out to me or to my family to check on me which means our friendship has no value to him.

Right before I came to jail, he started drawing one of the artists I invested a lot of money in away from me. Even though the artist spoke good about me and told Sean they would take care of me when they got a record deal, I knew that it was all talk. We had no contracts and even contracts aren't that protective these days.

I want all my friendships to be rooted in Jesus Christ. I want my circle to be believers with morals and godly principles.

OK, so back to Atlanta.

No one would have suspected what would happen a few days after I got there. As I was sleeping in my bed, I heard a lot of noise that sounded like banging on my door. I thought it was Sean trying to get in but it was my neighbors trying to warn me that our apartment building was on fire.

Even though Sean was my roommate, the place was in my name. I paid the majority of the bills and I had renters' insurance. You will understand why I make these points as we get deeper into this tragic event. Also understand that the mindset I have now is drastically different from the one I had before.

Thank God for the neighbors who woke me up because when I woke up, I could smell smoke and the ceiling in my room had started burning. Needless to say, they saved my life.

In my human mind I can't figure out why a lot of the events and tragedies happen in my life. When I allow God to take control things become very clear to me that I've been called to properly serve the Lord and bring others to the Lord.

No one lost their lives that evening in the fire but many lost their homes. Because I was planning to move, I had canceled my renters' insurance a couple of days before the fire. Also, Sean and I weren't seeing eye to eye on a couple of things which made me want to be myself as well. Moving back to LA was the best option for me. Sean didn't have much in the apartment but an air mattress and some clothes. Everything else belonged to me and our other roommate. Sadly, nothing was able to be salvaged after the fire.

I contacted the insurance company and filed a claim. Even though I canceled the policy, I was still covered for the month of December. The fire happened December 4th. Due to our losses, the insurance company expedited our claim and issued a check for a little over $9,000. At that time, I felt like no one was entitled to that money but me. So, I tried to lie to Sean and our roommate about receiving the settlement. Ofcourse, I got caught in my lie and reluctantly agreed to split the check three ways. Regardless, the money didn't mean that much to me. I had about 20k left from my other ventures.

Even though I was dating a few women in Atlanta, I planned to cut everyone off and start brand new when I got back home. After getting back to Los Angeles, I felt free again. I was still hurting over losing Kateri but I had to realize it was my fault we were over. I remember telling myself I would focus on my career and my daughter. I would get to know my son Joell, who I hadn't spent much time with since living in the south. Plus, I was upset that his mother didn't have an abortion like I asked her to.

I had a place to live with Monte, which was a good investment. We were both big on networking and we shared a lot of contacts.

My first month home flew by quickly. I was recording music with my younger brother, Tamrin and my friend and neighbor, Lil J. I was also enjoying my daughter and getting to know my son.

Christmas was a lot of fun that year. My family got to meet my son and his mother. My family loved him, but didn't care too much for her. Her attitude was bitter and very disrespectful when it came to me. She wanted more from me then I was willing to give at that time so we didn't see eye to eye. Regardless, we had a son and it was no longer about us. It was about him. We were both so stubborn. It would take much more to open our eyes. To this day, she's still stubborn but I can't make her change. I just have to be the best I can be for my children and allow God to work through me.

On Christmas, my brothers and I decided to go to Vegas for New Years. I invited Lil J and we all cleared our schedules to make this an epic adventure. I booked us a suite at the Wynn Hotel and bought a couple of cases of champagne to celebrate the new year. I also flew some girls in from Houston, just to spice up the environment. This was my first trip with my brothers without my parents and we really took advantage of that as well. Needless to say, we had an amazing time and brought in the new year with a bang.

Now we are in 2009.

So far this was the longest it had been without me going to jail. I was single and recording music rapidly. Lil J and I were becoming so close we decided to form a group called Mimosa. I was also spending a lot of time with Dsmoove and JC. We worked out together, partied together, created together, and just had lots of fun together.

Lil J wanted to move back to the valley so I asked Monte to find us a house in North Hollywood. This was around the end of February. By the beginning of March, Monte had found me a three-bedroom, two story home right off the 170 freeway and Sherman Way. This was perfect for us. A lot of recording studios were in this area. Hollywood was 10 minutes from us, which was perfect since Lil J was an accomplished actor as well.

Our last day in Vegas I met this beautiful young lady named Amy. Since meeting her and exchanging numbers I had been reaching out to her but she was playing hard to get. This girl was so beautiful, about 5'6", 125 lbs., long blond hair, amazing blue eyes and a perfectly fit physique. For some reason I couldn't get her off my mind but I became annoyed by her horrible communication skills. I also had so many local options in LA that I was able to put her to the back of my mind.

Then came Ciarra. Ciarra was the exact opposite of Amy. She was about 5'5", the same weight as Amy, with an amazing physique as well as perfect chocolate skin. I met Ciarra after a workout on Fryman Canyon. I had noticed her as we were running but I didn't say much. Then fate stepped in and as I was driving in the passenger seat of JC's Denali I looked to the right and noticed her driving. When I looked at her, she smiled. So did I. I rolled her window down and asked if I could have her phone number. She said yes and made my day. Ciarra was an actress/model who had just appeared in Jet magazine as their Beauty of the Week. She had recently moved to LA from Tennessee to pursue her dreams.

CHAPTER 7

As I sit here and think about all of these women I've loved and lost, it really sickens me. I know we are all sexual beings but I really think it's unhealthy for the human heart to try and love so many people in such little time.

It didn't take any time for Ciarra and I to become a couple. We had a lot in common and we were just so attracted to each other. Since our first date, we spent almost every day together for the first three months of our relationship. She met Ariyonna and Joell. She got along with them and all of my friends. My mentor, actor/comedian Miguel Nunez even got us to work on a pilot he was shooting as well.

I wasn't doing much to make money so I relied on Ciarra for a lot, which started to cause a little friction in our relationship. When these problems began, I started spending less time with Ciara so she wouldn't have to spend money on me. My ego was still high and slightly bothered by this so I started doing a few illegal activities here and there. Eventually, in the fall of 2009 Ciarra and I broke up. We decided to be friends with benefits. Ciarra didn't want to be sexual with random guys, so she would call me when she wanted to be intimate.

Then out of nowhere, Amy contacted me showing serious interest in me, which blew me away. She apologized for not communicating with me and of course, I accepted her apology. Since we met in Vegas, she had moved back to her hometown of Napa Valley and started going to nursing school. I shared with her how much I thought about her and suggested she drive down to see me.

By this time, Lil J moved out of my house and Big Dez moved in. Lil J and I had some differences over a girl who I had been intimate with for a few years. This girl had started being good friends with him and because I treated her so poorly, I was addicted to having a girlfriend to call my own. I also hated being alone which is one of the reasons my relationships failed due to me either cheating or being too needy.

Regardless, I didn't think I had a problem until now as I sit in prison with no woman writing me, visiting me, or supporting me. Now even though I've changed tremendously, I will still treat my future wife like a queen. This time, I won't be holding onto so much baggage and pain.

One of the blessings of being saved by Jesus Christ is the ability to cast my burdens on Him and know that I'm protected by His love and His blood.

OK, so back to Amy. Amy and I had a long-distance relationship but that didn't keep us from communicating regularly and confessing our love for each other. Even though she had no idea I was still being unfaithful. I was still seeing Ciarra and I had started dating this girl named Chaley that I met at LA Fitness.

This was the end of 2009 and Christmas and New Years were coming soon. Amy and I planned to bring in the new year together which gave me something to look forward to. I was still recording a lot of solo music and doing some odd jobs with Lil Man and a few friends from my teenage years. I wanted to do nice things for my daughter and my family as well as for Amy.

I did whatever I had to do to provide for them.

Christmas came and we had a great time as a family. My mother cooked a huge meal full of my favorites like sweet potato pie and deviled eggs. Everyone enjoyed their gifts and no one in my family was ever really aware of the monster I had become. I did a great job of keeping my street life away from my family's home. This didn't make anything I did right, but I was so numb by then, I couldn't open up and be honest about all my hidden personalities.

New Year's came and so did Amy. We really enjoyed each other and exchanged gifts. That night we went to an exclusive party on Paramount Pictures lot and we got pretty intoxicated. We really enjoyed ourselves but for some reason, we had a horrible argument on the way back home that got a little out of hand. By the time we pulled into the driveway, the words coming out of our mouths were very hurtful and we got in each other's faces. I accidentally head-butted Amy and she started crying.

Nowhere is it cool to get physical with a woman in any way but this honestly was an accident. This action caused everything else to stop. I instantly apologized to her and tried to comfort her. I was able to get her into bed, but when she woke up the next morning, she packed her things and left. I tried to talk her into staying so we could work it out but Amy was really hurt by my part in the horrible encounter.

Amy and I didn't talk for a week or two but eventually we reconciled and were together again. Amy was in nursing school and she really couldn't come see me much, so our relationship began to shift tremendously. That's when I started getting more serious with Cheley.

Cheley had recently got out of the military and she was currently unemployed but she still got a monthly check and she lived in LA. So not only was I able to see her often and quickly because she had a car but I could also see her almost every day, which made our relationship grow quickly.

Cheley was very different from the women I was used to. She worked out 5 to 6 days a week, she loved to drink alcohol and she was very aggressive. In the beginning of our relationship, this actually turned me on a lot. But after a few months of being together things started to get really intense.

Cheley would get drunk and try to fight me. She also fought a few of my close female friends. Not many of my friends liked her much. They didn't show her they didn't like her but they shared it with me privately, very often.

I was still living in North Hollywood in May of 2010 but was told I had to move because the bank was taking over my home. The bank offered to pay me to move, so I went apartment hunting. Of course, Cheley drove me to these appointments because I didn't have a car or valid driver's license.

That's when I met property manager Cindy Cooper, who was showing me a condo in Sherman Oaks. Cindy was a business woman in the entertainment world moonlighting as a property manager for one of her business associates. We started talking about each other's careers and goals. I told her I really needed this condo immediately. We said our good-byes and Cheley took me to lunch.

While we were eating, Cindy called and said I was approved and could move in immediately. This happened so fast. I knew Cindy made the decision off of our similar interests and connections. To this day, Cindy is still a close friend and supporter of my career. I'm very thankful to have this woman in my life.

The move went very smoothly. I went to Home Depot and hired a couple of guys who had a truck. We moved all of my belongings in a matter of hours.

Even though Cheley was technically my girlfriend our connection wasn't how it was in the beginning. She was extremely aggressive and she had a horrible drinking problem. Due to this turn of events with my feelings, I started searching for a new woman. I was still seeing Ciarra on occasion as well as Amy. I also had a few other women I was spending time with when I could but Cheley was possessive and hard to get rid of.

I was still using drugs and pursuing my career so I tolerated Cheley mainly because she did drugs with me and she would take me to the studio whenever I had a session. Our relationship to me was all about sex and convenience. What a bad combination, especially if you are seeking true love.

Even though I thought I knew what real love was, I really didn't. I was closer to real love as a teenager, but by this time in my life, at the age of 32, I was lost in lust, money, sex and drugs.

I really liked my new condo and so did many of my friends. I literally had 8 to 10 people living with me on a daily basis. We all did drugs and we were all entertainers. This environment was common in my world at the time. I knew many people who lived the way I did. There is no need to name drop, but just know that some of your favorite celebrities lived the exact same way I lived.

Not to justify it, or glorify it, but when you're on this side of this crazy world of entertainment, every day is one big party. I wanted to slow down and focus more but I just didn't know how to do it without letting down my friends. What was I thinking?

As I sit in prison not one of those friends who were living off me then are here for me now. Not one of them and it's so sad. Of course, I had issues, but I always had a big heart and I would go out of my way for so many people who never did the same for me.

I'm very thankful for these lessons and the fact that God has given me another chance after all I've done outside of his purpose for my life. We all have a purpose in life but not all of us realize our purpose because we were so busy doing too much that isn't right or godly. Yes, it's natural to be a sinner because of this temple we live in called flesh but we can defeat sin by accepting Jesus into our lives and allowing him to guide us down a positive and productive path.

This is not a religious choice. This is a lifestyle choice. Take religion out of the equation and see it for what it's been since the beginning. Do everything with love and just allow God to manifest many blessings in your life. I'm speaking from experience. None of this was taught to me. I live in the will of God.

As I continue this story about a lot of my life experiences and my many attempts at finding love, you will see consistently that God had a plan for my life. Through every struggle, He blessed me in many ways, so that one day I could share it with people who have lived just like me, or who are still living the same way I did and show them a better way to salvation. No one us are beyond redemption.

OK now back to the summer of 2010.

Me and Cheley were very close to being over. The only thing that kept us together were the things we needed from each other. She had a car and I had a condo. She didn't like staying with her friend in LA. She liked being with me in Sherman Oaks.

Due to her drinking problem, she had to go to jail for a few weeks for a DUI she received. This was a big relief for me because I needed a break from her. I had a couple of warrants for my arrest so I couldn't go visit her in jail, but she called me often. I was upset at her for not leaving her car with me so I used this time to really find some solid women.

Men and women are not as far apart as they seem. They cheat, they lie, they love, they cry, they hurt, they heal, they fall, and they steal.

We are all God's creation, but we all are not God's children.

I make this statement with pure conviction. The reason why I made these statements is because I've experienced all of the emotions I described earlier. I have made a complete change when it comes to the negatives mentioned. I've also realized how mad God was at me for not appreciating all that he has done for me and I made a choice to follow his principles and His laws.

But in 2010 I was so far from where I'm at now in 2016.

When Cheley went to jail I started planning my future based off of my next relationship. I put too much of my life into women and friends and not enough on myself. All of this made me a ticking time bomb set on self-destruction mode.

This was around the month of June. Cheley was in jail, I was doing lots of drugs with friends, and I was having sex with a handful of different women. I spread myself thin and started losing it all. My rent was past due, I had no money coming in, and I was just not mentally stable.

One of my friends in Atlanta, an actor named Sean Riggs, had a movie premiere in Atlanta. He invited me. I really needed to get away. I invited a couple of my friends who were involved in the white collar lifestyle like me, so we could do some shopping and get a limo for the movie premiere.

I was all about that fast life. Fast money, fast women, fast everything.

I had no steady pace of progression. I wanted it all now.

The flight to Atlanta was fun. We ordered a few drinks and flirted with multiple women on the plane. I was very excited to go to Atlanta for many reasons. I had a girl flying in from the Virgin Islands I met on FaceBook. She was so into me she offered to pay for my hotel room and get my teeth fixed.

As a child, I only went to the dentist twice because we had no form of insurance. I ate a lot of candy and didn't brush regularly. By the time I was in my early twenties I had a bad gum disease that caused many of my teeth to decay and fall out. This all happened before drugs, which was another reason why I did them. As a child, up until my senior year in high school, I had a perfect smile, which I took for granted and I thought would last forever.

In Atlanta, I had found a very good dentist with great prices I couldn't find anywhere else. I was actually referred to the dentist by my ex-girlfriend, Kateri's mother, Margie, who I was still in communication with.

This girl from the Virgin Islands was an attorney. She wasn't very attractive to me, but she was willing to help me out financially so I took advantage of this opportunity. I had done this to numerous women before and had done it to me as well. What a vicious cycle to live through.

Now I realize it's not good to use people at all unless your motives are rooted in love. But at this time, I was a mess. It was all about me.

When I got to the hotel, this woman already had two rooms booked, one for her and I and one for my friends. My friends were very impressed by the way I had set things up for us. This was my first time actually meeting this girl, but you couldn't tell by the way she treated me.

As soon as I saw her, she handed me money for my teeth. There was money for me to spend in Atlanta and to get another Blackberry cell phone, in addition to the one I already had. I had already set my dental appointment and arranged for Margie to pick me up and take me there.

The procedure was quick and painless. My new teeth were put in the same day. Now, my confidence was even higher because I could smile again. After we left the dentist, I took Margie to lunch and filled up her gas tank. She took me back to the hotel and I introduced her to Sean Riggs and my other friends.

After the introduction, we all went to this big hair convention in downtown Atlanta and did a little shopping with the credit cards. Lavell, one of my friends at the time, provided the cards. This was July of 2010, but in 2014 before I came to prison, he was killed in an after-hours on Vermont in Los Angeles. We were friends since childhood, but he lived a lot more recklessly than I did, but he was always a good friend to me.

We had fun shopping and meeting women all over Atlanta. The next day was the premier of Sean Riggs' movie that had Boris Kodjoe, David Banner, and one of the girls from *The Real House Wives of Atlanta* in it. We rented a stretch Hummer limo and showed up in style. I invited Miss Margie and the girl from the Virgin Islands but only me and the boys went in the limo. I had everyone else meet us there.

I could tell my distance bothered the girl because I didn't want to be seen with her. I feel bad about this now but I didn't think twice about it then and she dealt with it pretty well. At the premier, I sat with Sean Riggs, my boys and Margie but I had the girl from the Virgin Islands sit in the back of the theater with her sister she brought with her.

After the movie was over, we were invited to an after party. The limo was waiting right outside for us. Everyone saw us leave, including the girl from the Virgin Islands. I told her where we were going and I would see her later at the hotel room.

I was so hyper and excited because Sean Riggs actually played a very nice role in the movie. It made me proud and boosted my ego as well. We had a lot of fun that night and I met a lot of women.

When I got back to the hotel, the woman I was seeing was in a deep sleep because she was flying back to the Virgin

Islands the next day. Of course, I woke her up and made love to her. I wanted to make her feel better since I brushed her off so terribly earlier.

As I think about how I was before 2016, I don't even recognize myself. The man I am today is a mix between the cute little boy with big dreams and the well-seasoned man with a new heart for God and his children.

It was much easier writing when I first started but now that I'm getting closer to the present, I find it difficult to tell my story because I am so ashamed. I took so much for granted. I allowed evil ways to prevail. I was selfish, arrogant, promiscuous, on drugs, and money hungry. In a nutshell, I was just so worldly. But there's so much more to life than that. That's why I'm continuing this story.

I know many people have made a few or some of the same mistakes that I have made. They may think they're beyond redemption, but let me tell you a fact. It's never too late to turn your life over to God and treat all people with love and respect. That is why Jesus died for us all, to give us direct access to the Father and his mercy.

Like Philippians 4:13 says, "I can do all things through Christ who strengthens me." That's why I'm continuing my story in hopes that at least one person will be saved by my transparency. OK, so back to Atlanta.

The next morning, the girl from the Virgin Islands left to go back home. She gave me some more money and I pretended to really care about her but I had no intentions of seeing her again. She also booked the hotel for one more night for me and my boys who were leaving the day after her. As soon as she left, I pulled out my laptop and checked a few dating sites and my FaceBook account. That's when my love life took a brand new turn that would later change my life drastically.

As I logged into my FaceBook account, I noticed a request from a pretty and single Italian woman out of Westchester, Pennsylvania named Alysha. Alysha was a corporate woman with a strong college education and she was very interested in me. We instantly messaged each other and eventually exchanged phone numbers.

I don't really know why to this day, but I was very interested in her at the time. She was so nice and respectful. I enjoyed talking to and texting with her as well. I didn't really believe in long distance relationships but I was willing to try with her.

The next day we flew back to Los Angeles and Cheley got out of jail. She showed up at my house drunk and acting crazy as usual. I was pretty much done with her at this point, but I kept her around for various reasons. I continued to communicate with Alysha and we started getting really close, really, really fast. Then my life took another drastic change.

I was in the process of getting evicted from my condo. Cindy Cooper, the property manager, was actually on my side because the owner and I had personal issues. In the first week of August, I had a court date set to appear in front of a judge in the Van Nuys courthouse to fight the eviction. Cindy drove me to the court date and went with me into the courthouse as well. Cindy is an amazing person and I'll never forget how she was in my corner at such an early stage in our friendship.

The judge was actually nice and gave me an option to vacate the property in a few weeks and not pay a dime to the owner. She also canceled the eviction and stipulated that she would put the eviction in my name if I didn't vacate by the time she set. Cindy and I were very excited. This meant I could still get another place to live with no eviction hindering me. After court, Cindy took me to get my cell phone fixed and dropped me off at the condo. You will not believe what happened 15 minutes after she left. But of course, I'm going to tell you.

I got a knock on my door and I answered it. Standing there, was a man with a package that was supposedly in my name. He asked me if I was Oscar Roberts. I said yes. Then everything changed very quickly. He pulled out a badge and said that I was under arrest with warrants in multiple states. Before I could say anything else, I was in handcuffs and he and his partner were searching my home.

A couple of months earlier, my dog had a litter of puppies that were still in my care. When the police went into my room they were immediately met by my dog and a small army of babies.

I was very upset and confused because I hadn't gotten caught doing anything illegal since 2003 when I went to jail in Milwaukee. The officers didn't offer me much information. But they did tell me I would find out when I got to the Van Nuys jail.

What they did do for me was allow me to call Cindy Cooper to come get my dogs and my cell phones. They allowed me to call Alysha and tell her what was going on. Even though I had never met Alysha physically, something told me she would be in my corner. I also called my family but that was it for me. I didn't feel the need to call Cheley or any of the other women in my life.

At this point, I was still in a state of shock trying to figure out what I could have done to get arrested again. Finally, we got to the police station in Van Nuys. The officers processed me in and told me I had three warrants: one in Los Angeles County, one in Milwaukee, and one in Atlanta. I was so overwhelmed with grief; I began to cry and panic.

The officers gave me paperwork on my LA warrants and put me in a cell. This cell was like a mini dorm with about 20 bunk beds, a couple of toilets and a pay phone. I waited in line to use the phone. I called Alysha and told her everything I knew. Instead of pushing me away, Alysha offered to get me an attorney and get to the bottom of this.

I was so happy to have a woman in my corner that would help me, I started developing a stronger level of feelings, but they weren't from the heart. My heart was so tainted by then I couldn't really feel anything naturally, so I made myself believe these were feelings of love.

After a couple of days, I received a visit from a lawyer named Reza, out of Irvine, California. He told me Alysha retained him to represent me and that he was already investigating all of my charges. What he already knew was that the Milwaukee warrant was a parole violation for not paying my restitution. The Atlanta warrant was for a bad check. The Los Angeles warrants were accusations from different people who said I did something wrong to them.

One in particular was from my old investor, Gary. Apparently, his wife pressed charges about the Mercedes that I gave back and she added more to it, as well. Reza told me that it may take a couple of months but he would take care of all the Los Angeles charges. The out of state charges were beyond his jurisdiction. Even though I hated being in jail, I was very happy to have a real lawyer instead of a public defendant. I also had Alysha's support and my family, so I just let nature take its course.

Over the next few weeks, I got very close to Alysha. She wrote me letters and kept money on my books. After about a month of being locked up, I asked her if she would marry me when I got out. She said she would and told me that when I got out, I could come to Pennsylvania and live with her.

CHAPTER 8

Just like my new attorney promised me, all of my charges were dismissed. This all happened in early October of 2010. Now I had to wait to be extradited back to Milwaukee. Alysha and my family were very excited that the worst part of this battle was over. They also said they were trying to get the money together to pay my Milwaukee parole officer the restitution so I could get out as soon as I got there.

On October 18th or 19th, I was picked up by a private transportation agency, shackled from head to toe and embarked on what would be one of the most painful and horrible experiences I've ever been through. What should have been a two-day journey turned into a nine-day tour of the justice system. I went from Los Angeles to Arizona, New Mexico, Texas, Kansas, Missouri, Chicago and finally Milwaukee. We had to pick up and drop off prisoners to jails in all of these cities and states and sometimes, stay the night in these jails as well. By the time I got to Milwaukee, I was bleeding around my ankles and wrists.

A couple of days before I got to Milwaukee, one of my fellow inmates was able to smuggle his cell phone in. I was able to send Alysha a picture of us shackled in this small van. Alysha made a big fuss and called the heads of the company transporting us, but that didn't help at all. They took us to jail and had us strip search until they found the cell phone. Luckily, none of us got into trouble.

Shortly after that, we finally got to Milwaukee. I never thought I would be so happy to be at a jail but I was. This place was a holding facility for parole violators. I was processed in and given a cell then I called Alysha and my mom.

Alysha had sent my mom some money towards the restitution owed and my mom was still working on the rest. I wasn't really happy with my mom. I just wanted this to be over and she gave me an attitude, which really made me upset. Now that I think about it, I was wrong and very ungrateful but at this time I was just too arrogant. Having Alysha in my corner made me feel like I didn't need anyone else.

It took my mother almost two weeks to get the rest of the money together and I was released in Milwaukee. The warrant in Atlanta was still active, but it was a non-extradition warrant, which meant I could only go to jail if I came in contact with the police while visiting Atlanta. This whole jail experience from start to finish took exactly three months and one day. I was arrested on August 8th, 2010 and was released on November 9th, 2010.

After getting my property and my clothes, I called my mother to tell her I was released. I also told her Alysha wanted me to move to Pennsylvania with her. Even though my mother didn't have a personal problem with Alysha, she didn't like the idea of me moving. She wanted me to come home and continue to pursue my dreams. Then the conversation went left field. I hung up on my mother and called my father. That wasn't really a good idea, either. He got mad at me for disrespecting my mother.

Next, I called Alysha and told her everything that was going on. Even though Alysha had already prepared her home for me and made copies of the house and car keys, she unselfishly said that if I wanted her to do it, she would buy me a plane ticket back to California, instead of a flight to her home in Westchester, PA.

Even though I have no regrets in life, I have decisions I wish I would have thought more about and this is one of them. Because of my fear of having nothing and starting over alone, I selfishly decided to go to Pennsylvania. I thought I was in love with Alysha, but of course now I know it wasn't love completely. It was security, convenience, fear of being alone and some aspects of love but it wasn't love like a good woman like her deserved.

Alysha was the complete package; intelligent, beautiful, successful and confident. She was super into me and not the idea of me or what I could be. She liked the person I was at the time, which was a complete mess.

As I think about life now, I'm finally ready for a woman like that. Back then I wasn't mentally stable enough or spiritually in tune enough to appreciate and grow with a grown woman.

So, I took the bus to the airport in Milwaukee and like clockwork my flight was all set to perfectly leave in about an hour. I was very excited and nervous about this new mission I was about to embark on.

While I was waiting for my flight, I spent the whole time talking to Alysha. It felt good to be able to talk to her without the phone call being interrupted by the jail facilities time limit. Even though I had only known Alysha since July when we met on FaceBook, I had really made myself believe she was the one I was supposed to marry. If I didn't have multiple personalities that were out of control, this would have been very close to perfect but I was still a wild, sexually charged hustler.

Even though I believed in God, I was double minded. That type of mindset doesn't work too well for a believer. It's either you're in or you're out. There is no in-between with Jesus.

I boarded the flight with nothing but my cell phone and the outfit I was wearing. Alysha and I said our good-byes. She said she would be at the Philadelphia airport waiting for me when I arrived.

Readers, whoever you are and Alysha as well, please forgive me for the truth I'm about to share with you about this three-year journey from August 2010 to June of 2013. Some of the moments and experiences, as well as my state of mind were never fully revealed or admitted to Alysha. I was still in my own world. But now is definitely a great time to be completely honest with myself and this paper I'm writing on.

Now let me be perfectly clear by saying I've already asked God for forgiveness. I repented to him on my knees in prayer. But, like most of this story, it's been very therapeutic for me. I wish I didn't have to go to prison and be stripped away from my children, my mother, my father, my siblings and my dreams. I also wish I was in a more comfortable environment to write this story, but I'm not. I'm here in a Federal Correctional Institute surrounded by so many complicated minds that sometimes interrupt the fluid flow of this story.

I wish I could have started this when I had a cell but my heart was still healing from my ex-fiance who pretty much left me without a care. So I must endure my current position, living in a dorm, sleeping on a bunk bed.

This is my journey and I definitely see life more differently than I ever have before. I take the bitter with the sweet because, at the end of the day, I'm in prison because I was involved with illegal activities.

OK, so back to November 2010. Alysha picked me up from the airport on time. It had just snowed and the remains were still visible. The air was crisp and fresh at the same time. It gave my lungs much comfort but was uncomfortably tingly to my skin. The airport in Philly was only 30 minutes from our home in Westchester.

As soon as I saw Alysha, I gave her a big hug and lots of kisses. She didn't look exactly like she did in all of her pictures because of filters but she was still very nice to look at. Even though Alysha wasn't exactly my type, all of her other attributes made her quite appealing. This woman accepted me with all of my flaws. She opened up her entire life to me before even meeting me.

As she drove me home, she showed me a few landmarks like The Mint, where money is made and the small towns between Philly and Westchester. She told me about her dog, Asia and her two cats, Sammy and Amera. She loved animals. So, did I. That was a comforting similarity.

Finally, we made it to our home. Our place was nice and located in a nice sized community of townhomes. As soon as we entered the house, I was greeted by Asia but the cats never appeared. Asia and I got along great but the cats were very territorial. They came out for Alysha and that's it.

Since I had been incarcerated for three months and talking to Alysha about sex pretty often, we were both eager for what happened next. We really enjoyed each other and now she was officially my woman.

The next few days, Alysha took me to buy clothes and to get a Philly cheese steak. She worked full time as a supervisor for the American Red Cross and had been with the company for seven years. She had two degrees and a very complex life story, like mine.

She was Italian and never really knew her father. She had a brother and a sister and a pretty distant relationship with her mother because she always dated Black men. She loved her family a lot, but she didn't see them very much. Alysha was a loner, with a very small circle of friends that she barely spent time with. She worked very hard. Her previous mate had broken her heart and had a child while they were together so she lived her life much differently since him.

I didn't allow our love to flow naturally. I rushed everything. Not even a full month after I moved in, we were married. It was December 7th, Veterans Day. We didn't have a traditional wedding. We were married by a judge at a courthouse in Westchester.

I really took this woman for granted. It was all about me at this time. I wanted to be secure, I wanted to be loved, I wanted to be in control and I still wanted to do anything I pleased. Alysha treated me like a king and never stopped me from pursuing what I wanted. She often cooked me breakfast, and dinner when she got home from work. She was very trusting, which I wasn't used to. But after I realized the power I had over her, I changed into a very devious individual.

For Christmas, she got me a flight to see my daughter and my family. By this time, my mother and father were OK with our marriage as long as we were both happy. They were proud of me for making such a big decision and hoped my heart was in the right place.

When I went to California, I also connected with a new friend named Pint, from Northern California. We were both staying at the Ramada Hotel in Burbank. I met him in the parking lot and we smoked some marijuana together and shared some of our music together. He also told me he grew marijuana and he could set me up in Philly if I wanted to make some money.

Even though Alysha took great care of me, I wanted to bring in good money while I pursued my music and media dreams. I told Pint I was very, very interested and it was on from there. While I was still in California, I invited Pint and a couple of his artists to my studio session in Malibu at Krunchy Barn Studios.

Mike Williams was, and still is, the owner and engineer for the studio and a close friend of mine. Ever since Dawnmonique introduced him to me in the early 2000's we maintained a great friendship and music connection. I've recorded hundreds of songs with Mike and a lot of different artists over the years. Mike knew my sound and we would knock our records rapidly.

This particular session with Pint and his artist turned out great and we recorded a very catchy record. This was the beginning of a really strong friendship and business relationship as well. We trusted each other, which was a blessing because so many people are only out for themselves. But Pint was like me, not selfish at all.

It was time to go home to my wife and establish myself with some of the locals so I could provide them with my California essentials better known as Kush. I told my wife everything that happened in Los Angeles and about my new plans to sell marijuana in Pennsylvania. She had no problem with my new plans as long as I was careful.

A week after I got home, I received my first installment from Pint. It took me an hour to get rid of it and I profited a couple thousand dollars. Of course, my wife was happy and I was instantly hooked.

During my new drug dealing fiasco, Amy started contacting me a lot. She wanted me to leave my wife and move back to California with her. I still had strong feelings for Amy so I continued to communicate with her. I also let her know I just couldn't leave my wife.

I should never have got married. Why? Because the more I was with Alysha, the more I felt I could never leave her. She was too good to me. I wasn't really used to a woman as loyal as she was. She didn't check my phone. She didn't mind me staying out late or traveling. She truly loved me for me and I just wasn't ready.

As the months rolled by and my business grew, I started expanding my territory. I was recording music again and networking with people Miguel Nunez introduced me to.

Once a year, in June, a man named Charlie Mack has a special weekend where he invites a lot of celebrities and sports players to speak to kids in the neighborhood at this juvenile correctional facility. Miguel told me about it in advance. He wanted me to be a part of it with Vivica Fox and himself.

I told Sean from Cali about it and my boy Jerry, who owned one of the studios I was recording at in Pottstown, PA. The event was set for a date in June 2011. The exact date I don't recall. But I do remember the month.

By this time, I was doing business in Westchester, Philadelphia, Delaware, Baltimore, Virginia, Miami, New Jersey and all over New York City. I was making 30-50k a month.

My wife had no problem with anything I did as long as I came home as much as possible. This level of trust she showed me didn't help me remain faithful. Also, we were having a very hard time making a baby, which messed with my head even more. I was having sex with women in all of the states I did business in and I rarely used protection.

I purchased a firearm and hired a couple of guys to accompany me to all of my drops. They also possessed a firearm which gave me much comfort. Making money like that wasn't new to me but doing it in this fashion was because I wasn't involved in any white collar activities. I was a full-time drug dealer, a part-time rapper, and part-time husband. My wife had no idea the type of man I was becoming. I was living a double life and I really enjoyed it at this time.

Finally, the celebrity weekend approached and I met up with Miguel at his hotel. Miguel gave me a run down on how the weekend was planned and showed me the itinerary as well.

Sean was also good friends with Kai, daughter of actress Lisa Raye. Lisa was also a part of this celebrity weekend. We decided to meet up with Kai and her friends for dinner that night. I was also friends with Kai so we all had fun and caught up with each other. She really didn't believe I was a married man, especially due to my very flirtatious attitude towards her friends.

After we ate, we hung out a little bit longer, then we all said our good-byes. We were all aware of our very early schedule the next day.

Instead of going home, we decided to stay at the same hotel that everyone else was staying at in downtown Philly. I decided to stay with Miguel because I knew that he and Charlie Mack were very good friends and I wouldn't want to miss out on any of the plans.

The next day was a jam-packed chain of events. First, we had to organize all of the celebrities and get the police escorts in order. Our first destination was the juvenile detention center. Charlie Mack had about 15-20 SUV's prepared to transport all the celebrities and professional athletes.

Upon arriving at the detention center, I immediately recognized a football player I had met a few times before named Raheem Brock. He was currently with the Seattle Seahawks, but he was also a Super Bowl champion with the Colts, and a Temple University alumni. We started talking and he told me he had a record label called Beast Mode Entertainment. I told him about my company, Grind House Music Group and that I would love to build with him and create some magic for his artists. He was interested and we exchanged numbers.

During this conversation, Miguel and a lot of other celebrities spoke to the kids in the facility about following their dreams and doing positive things in their lives that would keep them out of jail. Then Raheem spoke.

A lot of the kids got excited because he was a Philly native. After everyone spoke, we were off to our next destination, which was like a fair/block party in one of the neighborhoods Charlie Mack was from.

Instead of riding in the SUV, I decided to drive on my own because I had my gun on me and a few ounces of marijuana for a client I was set to meet with later. I also offered to have Charlie's assistant as one of my passengers along with Sean and Jerry.

When we got settled at this event, I started receiving a lot of phone calls from customers needing product. I tried to avoid them all but one wanted to spend a couple thousand dollars with me. I couldn't let this money pass me by so I decided to take a quick drive to Delaware and get back to the event before anyone would miss me. I told Sean, Jerry and Miguel I was going to make a run. I didn't think anything could go wrong because of the day I was having.

I told the people I was meeting to meet me at the gas station right off the exit. The drive was swift and everything went according to plan. After the transaction was complete, I got in my truck and headed back to Philly. I was just at a gas station, but I didn't get any gas. I bought blunts and rolled a few up. Little did I know this would all come back to haunt me in just a few minutes.

After about 20 minutes of driving, my gas light came on. I was a few miles from the Philadelphia airport and a few more miles away from the event. Then all hell broke loose when my truck started to stall. I couldn't believe this was happening. I did the best I could to get to the side of the road.

I had previously been smoking marijuana and the blunt was still lit. I put the blunt out and called roadside service to help me fix this problem quickly. The operator told me it would take 45 minutes to an hour to get to me. I instantly began to panic because I had Charlie's assistant's purse and other people's property as well.

That's when I noticed a state trooper pulled over in front of me. He has just finished giving someone a ticket so I thought this would be an easy way to get help. I got out of the truck without thinking about my current state of mind and erratically approached the trooper.

Instead of helping me, he got aggressive with me. He got out of his vehicle and searched me. He could smell marijuana on me so he asked to search my truck. I became defensive. I asked why he was doing all this when I just needed help getting gas. He said he didn't care and asked if he could search my vehicle again.

I hesitated. I had weed in the car, a few thousand dollars, and a gun stashed in one of my bags.

The state trooper called for back-up and continued to search my truck. After he made a few threats, I submitted to his request. He searched the truck for a while. He eventually found my gun and money but he didn't find the drugs at the time. However, he found them later after he impounded the truck. After he found the gun, he put me in the back of his car and took me to jail.

CHAPTER 9

There are other elements of this story I could elaborate on but there's no point to it. I was wrong for selling drugs and carrying a concealed weapon as a felon without a permit. Once again, I caused myself to be pulled out of a beautiful business opportunity and behind bars again. The only difference this time was I was married and had money for bail and an attorney.

It took a day to get me in front of the magistrate who granted me a $25,000 bond. Once I got a bond, I called my wife, told her and she got me out two or three hours later. When my wife picked me up from jail, we went to get the truck out of the impound and she took me to meet my new attorney, James Lyons. I was so ashamed of myself I lied to my wife and told her the gun wasn't mine. But the reality is, it was mine and I was facing some time in prison.

This new attorney she found had a very good reputation and said he would fight for me the best he could. I felt good about him and I told him the truth and a lot of lies as well.

I just painted a picture of innocence for him and my wife. It really doesn't make sense to me now but at that time I was very selfish and stuck in my ways. My wife wouldn't have been mad at me regardless. But I lied anyway. After seeing my lawyer, I got right back to selling drugs. I had a consistent level of clientele and I was also addicted to making money the fast way.

My wife and I were trying to have a baby but the sex wasn't enough. She decided to do I.V.F. I didn't know much about this before, but over the next few months I became very familiar with this process. My wife had to inject hormones to make her produce more eggs and we had to have sex accordingly. If this didn't work then they would take my sperm and her egg, fertilize them and inject them into her cervix.

I was already a father of three children. I just couldn't understand why I couldn't get my wife pregnant with ease. That's when I really started sleeping with more women and traveling a lot more. I was stressed out and very insecure. Of course, my wife couldn't tell how unhappy I was because I kept my attitude in check when I was with her. But when I wasn't around her, I was a totally different person.

I had been going to Miami and New York a lot for business. I was selling weed and investing money in a friend of mine named Morocco who was directing music videos for Wacka Flacka and a new artist from the Bronx named French Montana.

Morocco and I had been friends for a few years but me moving to Philly and him living in Atlanta, just made things so much easier to do business. Towards the end of September, Morocco invited me to Atlanta to go to the Hip Hop Awards and we also had to finish shooting French Montana's video we had started shooting in New York.

I also had a song I wanted to shoot a video for as well. I put together a plan and consulted with my wife about it as well. As usual, my wife was OK just as long as I stayed safe and did things right.

I called my boy Pint in California. I told him and Sean to meet me in Atlanta. Sean decided to come to Philly and drive with me. Pint said he would meet me in Atlanta. I arranged everything else with Morocco and I hit the road with Sean and my young soldier Ahmad.

Living in Westchester made travel easy for me and enjoyable. New York was a two-hour drive, Delaware was a 20-minute drive, New Jersey was a 30-minute drive, Baltimore was a one- hour drive, Virginia was a four-hour drive, Florida was a 12-hour drive and Atlanta was just an 8-hour drive. I took advantage of the variety of cities at my fingertips and made my presence known in each town.

CHAPTER 10

My marriage was going well. My wife gave me lots of freedom. I was selling drugs to dealers all over the place including college campuses. I was recording a lot of music and connecting with various artists. My company, Grind House Music Group, was growing and I really thought my head was in the right place. But I was so, so wrong. I was so lost in my own world and thought nothing could really stop me. My supply was getting low which was good for me because I took so many chances driving from state to state with large amounts of drugs.

This was a good thing for this Atlanta trip because I needed to stay focused on the video, I was going to shoot with my artist Mil Sims from Pottstown, PA and the BET Hip Hop Awards. Also, Morocco and I had to finish shooting the Shot Caller video for French Montana.

While I was in New York with Morocco I invited my boy RAP from Ciroc to put the alcohol brand in the video. Due to French Montana's buzz in the industry and many networking avenues, Sean "Puffy" Combs attention peaked. Morocco told me that since the shoot in New York, Puffy reached out to do a cameo in the video and that's what we were going to shoot in Atlanta.

This all motivated me a lot and built my confidence even more. Even though I didn't know French Montana that well, I had developed a cool connection with him, his boy Chinx and Citi. These guys were true New Yorkers and French and Chinx were focused on music 24/7.

When we got to Atlanta, I decided to rent a condo in downtown Atlanta to stay and also shoot my video for a song called Trophy featuring Mil Sims. My business partner, Pint, was scheduled to land the next day, so I had to get everything in order before he came in from California. Morocco had a connection on BET Award tickets so I secured them for my whole team.

I have always been about making people happy even in my darkest days mentally. It's very strange to me now because I've grown so much more spiritually but I can see God building me and then preparing me for a mission only he could have orchestrated.

A lot of people living the way I was living either lost everything, died, went to jail for many years, and never reached positive success. But God's plan for me took me through segments of all of the attributes I described, but never to the point of no return. As sad as many of my moments in relationships with women, friends, and entertainment, God was preparing me for His work to be done accordingly.

The BET Hip Hop Awards was jam packed with excitement. I had my team in order. The condo was luxurious. Pint had a shipment delivered to the condo so he could make a little money and have a lot to smoke and share with the crew.

There was this girl named Christina that I had gone on dates with when I lived in Atlanta. She was a beautiful Hispanic woman with a great education. She was a stock broker and she had a place in my heart.

Even though I was married, I took her out on a date and asked her to play a big role in my music video. We made plans to shoot it after we finished with French Montana's video and the BET Hip Hop Awards. She said she would love to be in my video and my evening was made after her beautiful response to my request. I gave her the schedule and address to the condo and we enjoyed our evening.

The next day was the awards show and my boys were excited. Most of them had never been to anything like this or been to a video shoot like the one we planned for French.

This may make readers upset or even judge me but the basis of my story is truth and transparency. You see, in New York, when we shot the first part of the French's video, I had a couple of women with me. We had just spent a week in Miami doing some work for an escort service a female friend of mine set-up. In more or less words, I was a pimp as well, or a manager like others called it. Regardless, I was involved in helping these young ladies get money for sexual favors. During these escapades, I started developing strong feelings for one of these women named Evalynn. She was a very beautiful woman, Hispanic and French.

After we left Miami, I received a call from Morocco to go to New York and help him with the video. Of course, I had to go home to Westchester first and spend a few days with my wife and try to make a baby as well. I got a hotel for my two lady friends and went to see my wife.

I had been extremely sexually active with these two women during our trips to other states and while I was in Pennsylvania as well. So, by the time I got to my wife, I was spread thin. Of course, my wife knew nothing about my endeavors and I felt very guilty when I was with her.

There is no way to live such a foul lifestyle and still consider yourself blessed but I believed I was at that time.

So, we went to New York and shot the video. The girls were excited because they were fans of Wacka Flocka and French Montana.

In just a couple of months I was so connected to Evalynn that I quit the escort business. I continued to sell drugs and offered to take care of Evalynn the best way I could. She knew I was married and very understanding about my responsibilities. But this is where I went terribly wrong once again.

Right before I left to go to Atlanta, Evalynn found out she was pregnant. During this time, another girl named Clarissa had found out she was pregnant by me as well. As sick as this sounds, I was happy about Evalynn being pregnant, but I wasn't happy about Clarissa. I had only slept with Clarissa twice and had no real connection with her. That is why I felt so guilty for going to Atlanta without Evalynn because she was so used to being with me everywhere that I went.

Living this way as a believer in Jesus Christ is worse than a person living in sin who doesn't believe. Why? Because I am held accountable for everything that I did, because I knew better. But you couldn't tell that I knew better because I was living like a rock star/drug dealer. I had money, jewelry, women and friends but I didn't know myself at all. I was a ticking time bomb headed for destruction.

On the outside and on social media people thought I had it all figured out. But you will see as this story continues that we never have it figured out. And with God, all things are possible. Without him, you are headed for destruction.

After the Hip Hop Awards, I rented a stretch Hummer limo for the rest of the day. We had to go to the video shoot in style because Puff and Busta Rhymes were doing cameos and we wanted to blend in supremely.

Instead of missing my wife and wishing she was here with me, I was missing Evalynn. I called her to check on the baby and make sure she was doing well. I told her everything that was happening. I also called my wife to check in with her but my feelings were drifting rapidly. I was frustrated she wasn't getting pregnant. I blamed her because I had two women pregnant at the same time so I knew the problem wasn't me.

But now, God has shown me that the problem has always been me. I had very little patience. I wanted everything fast and now. Anyway, back to the story because things are about to change once again for the worse. And I'm still going to miss the message God has been calling me to receive for almost 20 years.

The video shoot went well and we got invited to Akon's club called Compound. I invited French and his entourage to ride with me and my crew in the limo. We went to the club and had a good time with Puff and T.I. I could tell by the way Puff was treating French that something big was about to happen in his career. Rick Ross was already on board so his path was being laid out right in front of me. After the club, I took French, Chinx, Uncle Murda and Citi back to their hotel. I picked up a few girls and took them back to the condo with me and my boys.

The next day we shot my video for Trophy featuring my artist, Mil Sims. Christina showed up on time and we had a couple of other women make cameos in the video as well. Everything went smoothly. Morocco put all my footage on my hard drive and gave it to me so I could get it edited. This was my first time shooting a video with a Red Camera so I was very excited about how it would come out.

Pint was set to fly back to California the next day and I was going to hit the road. My boy Sunny NY came and picked up some of the marijuana we had but he didn't buy it all, which left us with a few pounds. Pint was going to have it shipped to Westchester for me, but I told him I wanted to stop in Virginia and sell some to one of my cousin Andre's friends in Chesterfield. Plus, I was low at home and had immediate buyers waiting.

Basically, I didn't want to be patient and do things the safe way. I wanted to do things my way. So, I hit the road with my boys and set my GPS for Virginia.

Everything went according to plan. I got to my cousin's house in Chesterfield and his boy was waiting there for me to show up with the weed. Of course, he liked what he saw and decided to purchase a quarter pound to see what his customers would say. I gave him a good deal and gave my cousin a little bit for him to smoke as well. Before I left my cousin said, "Be careful. The cops are crazy around these parts."

I thanked him for the advice and asked where the closest gas station was. He told me I would run right into one before I got on the highway. I thanked him and said good-bye to him and his wife Sheeka, who is my biological cousin. Then I was off.

When I pulled into the gas station, I didn't notice a police officer pulling out because he had his lights off and I cut him off. I tried to hurry up and get to a gas pump to try and secure myself for any type of police contact but I was too slow.

This cop turned his patrol lights on and ordered me to get out of the car. He could smell the odor of marijuana so he searched my trunk.

He found the rest of the weed that I tried to stash in the back under the luggage. He put me in handcuffs and put me in the back of his car. He told Sean, Mil Sims and the other guys to get their property out of the truck because they were going to impound it.

I already had an open case in Pennsylvania that I was out on bail for.

Now I was about to have a distribution of marijuana case in Chesterfield, VA.

Of course, I called my wife. She got me a lawyer and bailed me out the next day. My aunt Tanya and Uncle Brad picked me up from the police station and took me to their house to wait for my wife to come pick me up.

Now I had two cases in two different states. I had two women pregnant and neither one was my wife. You would think that I would have slowed down a little bit- but no- I didn't. I speeded my lifestyle up and pretty much didn't care about anyone but myself.

My boy Sean was staying with my wife and I, and I was building a relationship with Raheem Brock and his record label. I found an editor to put my video together and linked him up with Morocco for direction.

My future son's mother, Evalynn had gotten her father to buy her a pretty nice Acura TL so I had more transportation. Evalynn was still under my care financially and we spent a lot of time together.

One day, I got a call from my boy Sunny NY. He told me he was going from Atlanta to his hometown in Rochester, NY and said he had some people he wanted me to do business with. I told him I was very interested. He sent me the address and I said I would see him in a few days. I told my wife and Sean. My wife said, "Be careful, please." Sean said he would make sure I didn't do anything stupid.

I called Evalynn and told her I wanted her to drive me and Sean to New York. She was excited because she loved taking trips with me. I called Pint and told him I was going to make a move in New York. He told me to be careful as well.

My biggest problem with all of my arrests was the fact that I was smoking marijuana while driving with either guns or drugs. It's a big no-no in the business I was in but many of us took the risk regardless because we were addicted. The day before we hit the road, Sean told me he would not allow me to smoke and drive. He said if I had to smoke, then we should pull over and I needed to get out of the car and do it. I said OK and packed a few outfits for our trip.

The night before we left, my wife and I made love again with the hopes of creating a child together. I really had a great woman but I wasn't mentally prepared or spiritually equipped enough to love her the way she deserved to be loved. Not many women would stick beside a man who kept going to jail and catching cases.

I know this because her and a girl named Jessica that I dated while living in Milwaukee were the only women to ever support me and communicate with me while I was in jail. Every other woman either left or hurt me deeply.

Most of my life I held resentment and painful memories close to my heart which never allowed me to heal accordingly. Now here I am. I'm married and trying to start a family but living multiple lives and thinking I'm going to be able to get away with it and succeed.

It's not like I didn't grow up with a beautiful example watching my parents love each other and serve God because I did. I just made horrible choices. I tried to use God instead of allowing God to use me and lead me down the right path. As you are about to see, my situation is going to keep getting worse even when it's looking like everything is going perfectly.

The next morning, I kissed my wife good-bye as she left for work. I sent a text to Evalynn to have her come pick me and Sean up. Evalynn was a little over three months pregnant and she had a little baby bump. As twisted as this sounds, even to me, I was super excited about this child. Out of all the women who had my children, I actually wanted this child and was involved with certain aspects that were similar to the moments I shared with baby Oscar that passed away.

Of course, I loved my daughter and had developed an amazing relationship with her, but I never met her until she was three years old. My other children lived in Texas, which made things difficult when it came to seeing them.

Because of the consistent let downs with my wife and not being able to get pregnant, I refocused my love and attention onto Evalynn. We were really going at a rapid rate.

Evalynn arrived at my home and we hit the road. I drove so Evalynn could rest. Sean sat in the back seat.

The drive to Rochester said a little over four hours on my GPS. About an hour after we were driving, I decided to pull over to smoke and get a snack at Burger King. I was so excited and a little nervous about getting to my destination safely that I couldn't even smoke the whole blunt I rolled. Of course, I didn't think wisely. I decided to wrap it in a napkin and put it in my pocket. Then we were back on the road.

We finally crossed state lines into New York. The city was called Binghamton, which I had never heard of before. It was a small city, from what I could tell from the freeway. I wasn't speeding, but for some reason, I attracted the attention of a New York state trooper. I couldn't believe I was about to be dealing with the police for a third time in less than six months. This had never happened to me before.

I didn't pull over immediately because I was so nervous. I just didn't get why this was happening to me once again. Sean and Evalynn were also pretty nervous, but there was nothing we could do this time.

I finally pulled over. The police officer asked me for my license and insurance. I gave it to him and asked why he pulled me over. He said it was because I had paper plates. He made a weird face and asked if I had been smoking weed. I told him I did earlier, but not while driving. He asked me to get out of the car. He searched me and found the half blunt I had wrapped in a napkin. He then asked to search the vehicle and I knew I was going to jail once again.

He found the few pounds that I had, impounded Evalynn's car, and took us to jail. I felt horrible because Evalynn was pregnant. I told the officers a crazy story and asked them to release Sean and Evalynn and let them go home. All the police wanted was me regardless, so they complied with my request and let them go. They also allowed me to give Evalynn money out of my wallet to get the car out of the impound.

That same day I was in front of a judge. I was charged with distribution of marijuana. I wasn't given bail. So much was running through my head. The worst thought I had was being in jail while married, with my one-year wedding anniversary approaching, and two babies on the way.

I finally called my wife and told her everything that happened. She told me she was very disappointed, but she loved me regardless. She would get me an attorney and let both of my other attorneys know I was in jail.

My attorney in Pennsylvania said he would take care of things and make sure my cases were postponed until my release. My attorney in Virginia said there wasn't much he could do. Once I missed my court date, my bail would be revoked and I would be extradited from New York to Virginia. This upset me tremendously. I felt like he was taking advantage of my being in jail so he could milk more money out of my wife and I.

The county jail in Binghamton was not much different than all of the jails I had been to before. I got along with everyone and stayed to myself most of the time.

The attorney my wife hired to take care of the case was known for getting men with cases like mine little or no jail time. When he came to see me, he was accompanied by a few other attorneys who were part of his team.

After discussing specifics of the case, he told me the officer had no probable cause to pull me over or even to search me. He said he would be able to get the distribution charge taken down from a felony to a misdemeanor possession. This news gave me lots of hope and motivated me to keep a positive attitude.

I called my wife and told her everything the attorney had told me. I told her I was very sorry for leaving her alone right in the middle of us trying to make a family. She told me she forgave me already and informed me that Pint would be coming to Pennsylvania to keep my clients satisfied and my cash flow going. I also called Evalynn and told her everything as well.

After a few weeks, I started writing a poetry book about my life experiences. I also started seeking God more but I was still double minded.

After about six weeks, and a few visits from my wife, my attorney made good on his word. He got the charges reduced to a misdemeanor possession and a $700 fine. Since I had already been in jail for 43 days, the judge gave me time served. He said to pay the fine as soon as I was released from jail and get my life together.

Now that this was done, I had to wait for Virginia to come and pick me up. It took about 30 days, but they finally came and got me.

They flew me to Virginia on the mayor's private little plane. This was the scariest flight I had ever been on. We could feel every inch of the wind, which caused an enormous amount of turbulence. We picked up a few other inmates from other facilities then we were finally heading to Virginia. When we finally landed in Virginia I had never been so happy to be on the ground in my life. I vowed to never, ever, fly on a small plane again.

After each of the inmates were accounted for, they separated us and I was escorted by an officer from Chesterfield County, Virginia. As we were driving to the jail, the officer told me that I would no longer have an outstanding warrant and I would be processed into the jail quickly. I could tell this experience wouldn't be as easily orchestrated by this attorney compared to the one I previously dealt with in New York. This attorney was more concerned about Chesterfield County than me and my immediate freedom.

My wife and I stayed in constant communication but I didn't get any visits because of the distance and also because she was working her job and taking care of my business the best she could.

I also talked to Evalynn often and received pictures of her as her stomach grew. In one letter, she sent me a few ideas and one of them really stuck out to me. Amiliano Julien. I thought this name sounded powerful and fit my son beautifully. I called her and told her my opinion. She agreed with me and said she would name him that.

I talked to my family a lot and got a couple visits from my Aunt Tanya and Uncle Brad.

I was very lost emotionally during this time in jail. I had so much guilt and ill feelings about my life that I was suicidal at times. I thought about taking my life and saving everyone in it a lot of pain and embarrassment.

I tried seeking God as much as I could, but my heart was never really in it. I just wanted to be free and be able to hustle and do music. That's all I cared about. My wife was becoming further and further from my mind. I knew I had destroyed our marriage, but I didn't have the guts to tell her.

I spent Christmas and New Years in jail once again. I spent my first wedding anniversary and another birthday incarcerated. Now it was 2012 and I was getting closer to resolving my Virginia case.

Shortly after my birthday in March, my attorney came to visit me. He said he had a plea deal for me. The deal was a 5-year sentence with 4 years and 8 months being suspended. The deal pretty much meant I would be getting time served once I got in front of a judge.

During this time in jail, I wrote a poetry book. I had been writing poetry since I was a child, but I had never put together a body of work like this until I was incarcerated.

My court date to accept and sign my plea agreement was the first week of June. This was the longest I had been in jail since Milwaukee. I didn't really learn much because I was battling against so many personal demons and past issues. They made me a bitter and resentful individual.

I was now the father of five children, from five different women and married to a great woman I didn't respect or appreciate. I should have told my wife the truth then and saved her from heart break but I didn't because I was selfish. I was scared of being alone which really makes no sense to me now but in my transparency, I must be honest with my life.

I want to help others who are dealing with similar issues and are afraid of being honest. Lies are not the answer. Lies only make matters worse, but the truth will set you free.

My court date came and I was out of jail the same day. I had built a friendship with one of the correctional officers. He told me he would pick me up when I got released and take me to my Aunt Tanya's house in Richmond, Virginia. His brother was a music producer and he felt I would be a great outlet for his music. He said he would bring a CD with some of his music so we could listen to it while we drove to my aunt's house.

This all turned out to be a great connection because his production was great. I instantly came up with songs as I listed and I had a great connection to them as people.

My wife was already on the road to come pick me up from Richmond as well.

Once I got to my aunt's house, I introduced my new friends to them. We said our goodbyes and planned to connect after I got settled at home in Westchester. I always had a great time when I was with my aunt, uncle, and their lovely children. I really wish we lived closer when I was growing up because our bond is just super strong. After spending a few hours with them and catching up on old times, my wife showed up.

I couldn't wait to give her lots of affection and sleep in my own bed. My wife was so good to me and very special but I really couldn't match her accordingly. She deserved for me to be the man she fell for back in 2010.

When she picked me up, she made me aware of certain things that couldn't be said over the phone about Pint and the people I had working for me. Once again, I was free and able to keep building my empire and I only had one pending case left to fight.

Ironically, the infamous Charlie Mack weekend was coming up again and my friend Raheem's birthday as well. Even though I was still involved with illegal activities, I decided to slow down a little and focus on my career and my relationships with those who had similar dreams.

My wife still wanted a child. Since the hormone therapy didn't work, we decided to try in vitro fertilization. This is where the doctor takes her eggs and my sperm, inject them close to the uterus, and hope it will be a success. I had many reservations because my love for her wasn't the same and now I had two new children to provide for that were both created during my marriage.

Even though I know God has forgiven me and I'm finally aware of who I am as a believer, I can't help but feel guilty from time to time. Especially now that I'm sitting in federal prison, serving the most time I've ever done. There is no woman by my side. I'm disconnected from my children and watching most of the people I've called friends succeed in this entertainment industry. I'm also physically tainted and humbled by everything I've done. It's going to take an amazing, God fearing woman to love me as I am.

I'm not as inspired to write as I was when I first started telling my story. The main two reasons are these prison walls and the painful memories that occurred between 2012- 2016. This part of my life made so many wrong turns, it's a miracle I am here to tell it. Anyway, back to 2012.

I was able to get my truck back that was impounded, but I wanted something new so I got a 5 Series BMW. While I was incarcerated my wife traded in my Lexus and got a Kia Optima, fully loaded.

I started seeing both of my son's mothers and also became sexual with them again. They both knew I was married but they didn't care because I didn't care, either.

EPILOGUE

This year was a very risky year for me because I felt I could do anything I wanted to. My wife didn't restrict me and the circle I was in was very successful. I would go to New York and network with my good friend Skitzo who is a producer and artist. I was doing A&R work for Beast Mode Entertainment and traveling with them all over the country shooting videos, doing shows and recording music with a lot of my friends in the business.

I felt accomplished most of the time, but I was never fully satisfied mainly due to the fact that I had dreams and personal goals I had to put on the back burner to help the different artists I was managing.

Now, when I reflect on everything, I realize God was calling me to do what he wanted me to do and He wanted me to leave a lot of the people I was dealing with alone. He wanted me to change my ways. Even though I had good intentions at times, they don't mix with a sin-filled life.

My wife and I were growing further apart, mostly because she wasn't getting pregnant. The process with the doctors made it very stressful for both of us. Also, my lifestyle didn't help at all. I was barely at home and I was dealing with so many different women, which wasn't fair to my marriage.

No one should get married unless you are prepared to be honest, transparent, and loyal at all times. You also shouldn't get married if you don't really know the person you claim to love. You don't have to wait years, but at least build a solid foundation and grow from there.

It's sad to say but the truth is I never really loved my wife. I got married because I didn't want to be alone and because it was convenient. These are horrible reasons to get married and I hope I can save some people a lot of heartache and pain through my story.

I still had many opportunities to come clean, but I was too selfish and arrogant during this season of my life. I was making my own money, I provided for my wife, and I provided for my children as much as I could. I really felt that I was entitled to do what I wanted. I was so good at changing my personality that my wife thought I had a good man. Of course, I was good to her, but that doesn't count when you're living a double life.

It felt good to spend our 2nd anniversary together, instead of being behind bars like I had been the year before. We went to the Port in Maryland and had a romantic dinner. Then we went to Ocean City and spent a couple of days laid up on the beach.

They say that a man that is faithful sometimes, isn't faithful at all. I really didn't appreciate all that my wife did for me and the sacrifices she made for me when I was fighting all of my cases. She deserved a man to be all about her and I wasn't at the time. I still had so much to learn about myself.

I had to release a lot of baggage from past relationships and experiences that had a traumatizing effect on my life.

By the end of 2012 and the beginning of 2013, my love for my wife had evaporated. I was always on the road trying to make as much money as I could. I was no longer interested in being married. I had so much guilt from cheating on my wife so much and having two children out of wedlock.

I know God was very unhappy with the lifestyle I was living and I honestly didn't care. I thought I was special in God's eyes- so special that I could live any way I wanted to and I would still be blessed and successful. Of course, I knew better, but I didn't do better. I neglected all of the home training my parents showed me in their love filled marriage.

In March of 2013 I was arrested again for possession of two firearms. Two of my friends and I went to Atlanta to see some women and make some money. I had just spent my 35th birthday with my wife and things were looking up. But I was still a selfish dirt bag and I was in for another bunch of surprises.

During these few months in Lawrenceville, GA my wife filed for divorce.

I realized a lot about myself and I decided that when I beat this case, I was going home to my family to start over. That's when I met Cristal, the woman I just knew I was going to spend the rest of my life with.

Cristal and I met through a mutual friend who was an actor. They were actually dating when I met her but their relationship wasn't serious. The day I met her the connection was very strong and I was instantly on a mission to make this woman mine. I asked my friend how serious their relationship was and that was when he told me that they were just friends with benefits. You would think I would have paid attention to the signs that were given to me then but I followed my lust filled eyes and pursued her anyway.

I met Cristal in the winter of 2013 but I didn't see her again until the spring of 2014. One of my friends was on a social media site called Instagram and he reminded me about that fine ass Hispanic girl our mutual friend used to date. He also told me that she was not dating him anymore and that he planned to pursue her.

As he was going over her Instagram profile, I memorized her screen name and sent her a friend request from my Instagram account. Within minutes she and I were having conversations and that's when I told her how I had thought of her often since we met. I also told her that if she would give me a chance I would make her a very happy woman and treat her like a queen. That night she came over to my house and that was the beginning of our toxic love filled relationship. This woman and I fell deeply in love so fast it was scary and we went through so many ups and downs in such a short amount of time.

In less than a year, this relationship took so much out of me that I'm not going to really give it too much life. It ended with her leaving me while I was in prison writing her letters every day confessing my love for her and asking for just one chance at a love I had longed to experience.

This woman did so much to hurt me while I was incarcerated, I would have to write a book just about that but in a nutshell, she destroyed my heart and started sleeping with a very close friend of mine who I considered a brother.

I realized so much about myself in going through this and I learned how to love myself completely. I also became bitter and extremely emotional after going through all of this but I'm so much better now. I'm really blessed in so many ways. My career is rebuilding very fast and I really love myself so much I refuse to settle for anything less than what I deserve.

After serving 28 months in federal prison for receiving stolen artwork that crossed state lines and getting over 50 months taken off of my sentence for saving my cellmate's life after he slit his wrist and throat in front of my face in the middle of the night. I'm a changed man. Of course, I still have much to learn about life and love and the pursuit of happiness. I can't help but be thankful for each and every experience that I've been involved in because it has made me a very strong and focused human being.

This story is personal. This story is real. This story is my testimony. This story is to heal. This story is to teach. This story is to reach. This story is so much of me. This story is me going through the battles of life and love and pain. This story is a formula for many to learn from and hopefully help influence change.

I've lived. I've loved. I've done it all, some would say. As for me, I haven't done enough on my mission to find my way.

Thanks for being a part of my story and I hope I didn't offend anyone with all the truth I've exposed. God bless you all and have an amazing day.

Printed in the USA
CPSIA information can be obtained
at www.ICGtesting.com
LVHW011641240224
772712LV00064B/1651

9 781963 254082